WINNING
IN LIFE

30 DAY DEVOTIONAL FOR BUILDING
STRONG FAITH

WINNING
IN LIFE

For Teens & Young Adults

David S. Winston

Illustrations and Design by TheLittleLabs Studio

Winning in Life: 30 Day Devotional for Building strong Faith for Teens & Young Adults
Illustrations & Design © 2024 TheLittleLabs Studio
ISBN: Print 979-8-9914331-0-5 | eBook 979-8-9914331-1-2

David S. Winston
7600 Roosevelt Rd.
Forest Park, IL 60130
davidswinston.com

*I dedicate this book to my dad, who is my hero
and taught me faith from a young age.
Thank you, Dad, for our years of Bible studies
at the dining room table. I am forever grateful.*

*Also, to my wife Niki. Your love and support make
everything I do possible.*

INTRODUCTION TO THE JOURNEY OF FAITH

Welcome to this journey of discovering the power of faith and how it can help you win in life. Whether you're facing the pressures of school, navigating friendships, or figuring out your future, having faith in God is your ultimate game-changer. This devotional book will guide you through understanding, growing, and living out your faith daily. It's a playbook to show you how to live a victorious life.

When I think of the word victorious, I think about winning teams. Winning teams have things in common, such as winning game plans, mindsets, and habits. That means they study how to win. They think about how to win. Then, they practice the skills and develop the behaviors necessary to win. Fortunately, you don't have to be a professional athlete or a competitor to understand what it takes to win. We all have experienced what it takes to overcome challenges to win at something.

The good news is that God wants you to win in life. Your ability to live a victorious Christian life as a young person depends on your thinking, behavior, and habits. If you allow God's Word to shape all three, you will win in life. Fortunately, God has given you all the tools to be victorious, but will you use them? That will determine the victory.

God has already promised victory through Jesus Christ so you can win against anything life or the enemy would try to throw your way. In 1 Corinthians 15:57, the Bible says, "But thanks be to God! He gives us the victory through our Lord Jesus Christ." The ability to win has already been granted to you through what Jesus did. It takes having faith in God to make winning our reality.

You'll face many unique challenges and opportunities as a teen or young adult. The world often sends mixed messages about what it means to be successful and happy. But God's Word provides the proper foundation for winning in life. It's not about fame, wealth, or popularity; it's about living a life that honors God and reflects His love to those around you.

In this book, we'll explore what it means to have faith in God and how that can transform every aspect of your life. From dealing with anxiety and trusting God in hard times to building solid relationships and pursuing your dreams, you'll find practical advice and biblical truths to help you navigate life's ups and downs. Faith isn't just about believing in God; it's about trusting Him with every part of your life. This devotional will teach you to live by faith and get good results!

Each devotion is relatable and encouraging, with real-life examples and Scripture-based revelations. With a daily foundation scripture and a couple of pages of insights, you'll learn how to trust God more deeply, seek His wisdom, and lean on His strength. Through daily reflections and prayers, you'll discover that faith isn't just a one-time decision; it's a journey of growing closer to God and becoming who He created you to be. Take time and reflect on each topic. Write your thoughts down in this book. It will help you not only set an expectation for what God will do, but it will help you document your journey of growth.

Before you begin, take a moment to ask yourself: What do I want to see change in my life? What am I believing God for? How do I want to grow? Get ready to dive in and let your faith soar! Remember, with God on your side, you have everything you need to win in life. Let's embark on this adventure together and watch how God transforms your heart, mind, and future through the power of faith.

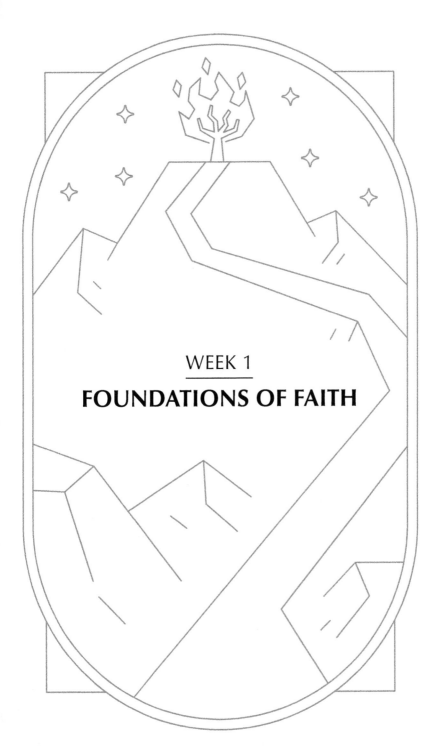

WEEK 1

FOUNDATIONS OF FAITH

Now faith is confidence in what we hope for and assurance about what we do not see.

Hebrews 11:1

DAY 2

WHAT IS FAITH?

Look at your shirt. You know that it's real because you can touch it. Look at your smartphone. You can feel that, too, and see that it's real. You know it's real because your senses tell you so. No one can convince you that it doesn't exist. It's easy to believe in what we see, but it can be much harder to believe in something we don't see. Have you ever had a friend tell you something that seemed too strange to be true? Because you didn't see it for yourself, you had to choose to believe it or not. God's Word and His promises are the same way. God asks us to believe in His promises that we cannot see. That is faith.

When the Bible mentions the word faith in the New Testament, it means to be divinely persuaded. This divine persuasion is not just a belief, but a deep assurance that God is who He says He is, He's going to do what He said in His Word that He would do and that He will do it for you. This assurance, this faith, is what guides us in our journey. Hope and faith operate a little differently. Hope is a confident expectation that God can do something. Faith is when you are fully persuaded that He will do it for you. If you were to cook a meal, hope would be buying the groceries. However, faith goes a step further, bringing the ingredients together and preparing the dish so that it is ready for consumption. That's called the manifestation of your faith. These two elements work together. Where there is no hope, faith cannot exist.

We allow our faith to take root when we believe in God and His Word. The Bible says that we are saved by faith. The only way we can receive the gift of salvation that Jesus died to provide is by faith (Ephesians 2:8–9). Additionally, all of the other great things that God has promised us (healing, peace, prosperity, wisdom, direction, purpose, etc.) must be received by faith. When we put our complete faith and trust in Jesus, we can live a life that is pleasing to God and filled with His blessings. This is called the abundant life, as Jesus mentions in John 10:10, which is meant for you!

Faith isn't just about accepting the truth of who God is; it's about actively living out that belief daily. This means trusting God in the big and small decisions and expecting His goodness in every situation. As a young person, you're at a point in life where decisions carry more weight, and your challenges can be more complex. Whether it's overcoming personal limitations, choosing a college, pursuing a career path, or dealing with relationships, faith is about leaning on Him when life gets tough and knowing that victory is yours.

Lastly, faith means being patient and persistent, knowing God's timing is always perfect. As you grow in faith, you'll discover a deeper sense of peace and purpose. Remember, faith is not a one-time decision; it's a daily commitment to trust and follow Jesus, even when the road ahead seems unclear. This commitment to faith, to patience, and to persistence is what will carry you through the challenges and uncertainties of life. Through faith, you open the door to experiencing God's miraculous power in your life.

PRAYER

Lord, I commit today to live a life of faith. I will not cast away my confidence, but I will believe what Your Word says. Help me to remain steadfast in Your promises for my life. When challenges come, help me to see Your promises manifested in my life. I will not doubt. I will believe You! In Jesus' name, amen.

REFLECT

Are there any areas in your life where you have given up hope? As you write down any situations, describe why you have lost hope. Commit those areas to God for a turnaround.

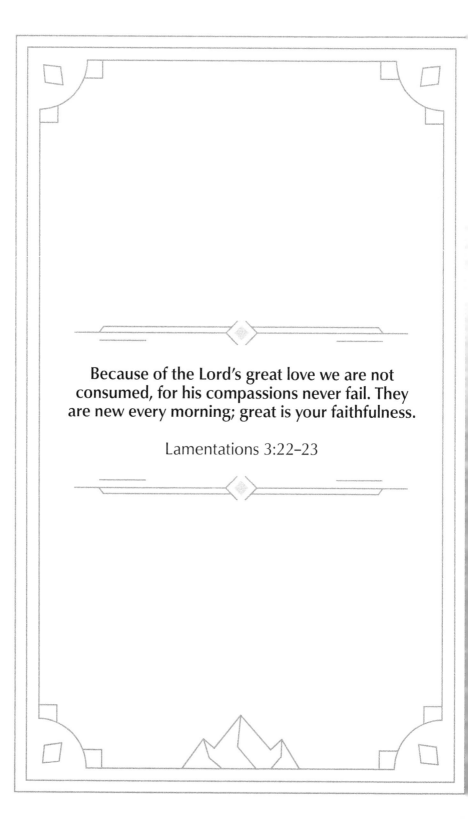

Because of the Lord's great love we are not consumed, for his compassions never fail. They are new every morning; great is your faithfulness.

Lamentations 3:22–23

DAY 3

GOD'S FAITHFULNESS

Have you ever had someone break a promise? Maybe they said they would do something for you or show up on a particular day and time but left you hanging. I've had it happen to me, too. It's so frustrating. But the good news is, God is not like that. You can trust God to keep every promise He has made to you. That's faithfulness. In a world where human reliability can be shaky, God's integrity is unwavering. He is reliable, loyal, trustworthy, unwavering, and steadfast in His behavior.

When we read today's verse, we are reminded that God's faithfulness is unparalleled! It is far better than anything we have experienced in our natural relationships with parents, family, or friends. If you don't have many people in your life who can be trusted, know that God's faithfulness stands alone, unmatched by any human relationship.

In many years of working with youth, I've noticed that they often see and experience God similarly to how they see and experience the most important relationships in their lives. They may have difficulty trusting God if they have trouble trusting other important people in their lives (especially if those people are untrustworthy or disloyal). They must learn that God's behavior is unlike the unreliable behavior of others around them. If you are one of those people, know that God can be trusted; faith in Him is how you exercise that trust. The Scripture says that God is not a human that He should lie or change His mind (Numbers 23:19). If He says something, you can depend on it.

Our world is in a constant state of flux. Music styles, clothing trends, technology, and even political leaders come and go. But in this ever-changing landscape, God's faithfulness remains a steadfast constant. The Bible tells us that Jesus is the same yesterday, today, and forever (Hebrews 13:8). His promises to you are as true now as they were the day you received Christ. You can always rely on God's love, direction, and strength to guide you through life's changes.

As a teenager or young adult, you're in a season of change. Your interests, friendships, and even your identity are in flux. It can be overwhelming not knowing what to expect next. But in this uncertainty, God is your constant. He's the anchor that holds steady when everything else is shifting. When you feel you can't count on anything else, you can always count on God. He is your rock, and His promises are a firm foundation on which you can build your life. Trusting in His unchanging nature will give you the confidence to navigate life's ups and downs, knowing that He is always faithful to His Word.

PRAYER

Lord, help me to see Your faithfulness every day in my life. I know that You cannot lie, and I trust in who You are. I praise You that Your faithfulness endures for all generations. I ask that You would be an anchor to my soul. Even when others leave, I know that You will never leave me or forsake me. Thank You, Lord, for always being with me. In Jesus' name, amen.

REFLECT

Write down what it means for someone to be trustworthy. What are some areas in your life or some situations that you have already seen God prove His faithfulness?

For by the grace given me I say to every one of you: Do not think of yourself more highly than you ought, but rather think of yourself with sober judgment, in accordance with the faith God has distributed to each of you.

Romans 12:3

DAY 4

WE HAVE GOD'S FAITH

As we talk about faith, we must know where faith comes from. Have you ever wondered what the origin story is for our faith? The faith that we have is something that God has given to us as a gift. It did not originate with us. There is a passage in the Bible where Jesus curses a fig tree; these trees can grow to be rather large. The day after Jesus had spoken to that fig tree, He and the disciples passed by it again, and they noticed that it had completely dried up from the roots–a process that naturally would have taken months. (See Mark 11:20–24.) Peter pointed this out to Jesus, whose response was simple: Have faith in God. The original translation of this statement reads, "Have the faith of God," or we can put it this way: Have God's faith–a faith that is unwavering and powerful.

As you reflect on today's scripture, you may be asking: How much faith has God given me? Did He give me enough faith? Does He give all of us identical amounts of faith? Some translations of this verse imply different amounts, and some translations state "the" measure of faith, leading one to believe that we all have the same amount. Let's look back at the historical Roman culture for a better understanding.

In the Bible, the apostle Paul (the writer of the Book of Romans) refers to faith as being like a shield (Ephesians 6:16). The Roman soldiers of that time were usually provided with shields that were custom-fitted for them. The size of the shield depended on the size of the person. A short man would have a smaller shield, and a taller man would receive a bigger shield. I believe this is how God has dealt His measure of faith to us individually. He has given us the exact amount of faith we need to do what He's called us to do. He's given us the right amount of faith that we need to win every battle in life.

But let's go one step further. When Jesus challenged the disciples to live with a higher degree of forgiveness, they responded by asking Him to increase their faith. Perhaps they thought they did not have enough faith to accomplish the task the Messiah had given them. His response told them that if they had faith the size of a mustard seed, they could do what seemed to be impossible (Luke 17:1–6).

Consider the mustard seed, one of the smallest seeds. Jesus uses this as an example to show that even a small amount of faith can achieve mighty things. The disciples didn't need to acquire more faith from Jesus; they had enough for the situations at hand. They just needed to use it properly. As you use the faith you've been given, it will only grow stronger each time you use it. Your faith in God will always lead you to victory because you have God's faith, and His faith never fails.

PRAYER

Lord, help me to use my faith effectively. Help me to use my words to speak life and not death. I thank You for giving me all the faith that I need to win every battle. I know with the faith You have given me, I cannot fail. I will use my faith like a shield to successfully fight off all the attacks of the enemy. Thank You for giving me YOUR faith! In Jesus' name, amen.

REFLECT

How do you think you can use your faith more effectively?

Trust in the Lord with all your heart and lean not on your own understanding; in all your ways submit to him, and he will make your paths straight.

Proverbs 3:5-6

WEEK 1: FOUNDATIONS OF FAITH

DAY 5

TRUSTING GOD
IN UNCERTAINTY

This verse, my favorite scripture in the Bible, has been a constant source of reassurance in every season of my life. It's a comforting reminder that God always has a plan for me, even when I can't see it. And if you're not in that season yet, rest assured–it will come, my friend.

This scripture is so close to my heart because it provided the reminder that I needed when I was confused and frustrated about which way to go. I was in my last year as an undergraduate student at Oral Roberts University. I wanted to become a doctor, specifically a heart surgeon, so I needed to apply to medical schools as my next step after getting my bachelor's degree. Over the next several months, as I applied and received responses, I kept getting rejection after rejection. It was a tough time for me, and I felt like my dreams were slipping away. Doors of opportunity kept closing fast all around me. My whole life I had wanted to become a doctor, but I couldn't do that if I couldn't get into medical school.

By the time I got the last rejection letter, I was freaking out. I was feeling uneasy, trying to keep my faith up in the midst of uncertainty. I would meditate on Proverbs 3:5–6 to remind myself that God would give me direction. I soon went to a young adult conference at the church I was attending at the time, and God met me there in a powerful way. It was a night I'll never forget. As I cried out to God at the altar, He spoke to my heart and told me that I had planned to heal hearts in the natural, but He had planned for me to heal hearts spiritually. Long story short, He told me His plan for me was to go into full-time ministry and minister to the young generation. The reason why I'm writing

WINNING IN LIFE   23

this book today is because of my encounter that night. I trusted that God had a plan, even when I couldn't see the blueprint. As of the writing of this book, I've been pastoring youth and passionately ministering to people for fifteen years.

Let this verse today become the anchor of your faith. Declare this scripture out of your mouth daily. As you do, you will grow your faith, expectation, and sensitivity to receive God's direction. Confident faith will replace doubt. I believe that because I meditated on this scripture, my faith grew to receive God's direction and put me where I would hear His voice. As you seek direction from God, refuse to lean solely on your understanding. Trust that God has a better plan than you could imagine.

As a young person, you're standing at the crossroads of countless decisions—what college to attend, what career to pursue, who your friends are or who to date, and even what kind of person you want to become. It's easy to feel overwhelmed and unsure, but this is where faith steps in. When life feels uncertain and the future seems blurry, remember that God's plan for you is already laid out. He sees the bigger picture you may not see yet, and His timing is always perfect. Lean into that assurance and take comfort in knowing that the One who created you has every detail of your life under control. You don't have to have it all figured out. Simply trust the One who does.

PRAYER
Lord, as You promised in Your Word to give me direction when I trust in You, I commit to trusting You today. I receive Your direction, Lord. I refuse to be prideful. I ask that You would show me where to go, what to do, and how to do it. Direct my steps each and every day. In Jesus' name, amen.

REFLECT

What situations are you facing right now where you need God's direction? What are some of the things that you are tempted to trust in when you should be trusting God? What are some of the ways or methods that God can use to direct you?

Do not be anxious about anything, but in every situation, by prayer and petition, with thanksgiving, present your requests to God. And the peace of God, which transcends all understanding, will guard your hearts and your minds in Christ Jesus.

Philippians 4:6–7

DAY 6

THE PRAYER OF FAITH

Several years ago, we went on a cruise on one of the mega-cruise ships. Standing on the dock next to it makes you wonder how we could build something that big that actually floats on water. To move a ship that size, it takes an equally impressive engine—in fact, several huge ones. As big and fancy as those billion-dollar ships are, they won't move unless something powerful moves it.

Prayer is the engine of your faith. It gives your faith the strength and power to move forward. Prayer invites God to manifest His promises in your life. I believe this is why the Gospels mention how many times Jesus went away to pray. His strength was being renewed, His faith was being empowered, and His discernment was being sharpened. You are the same way. You cannot survive spiritually without prayer. Your faith would grow weak, and life would overwhelm you. But through the transformative power of prayer, you can find hope and inspiration to face life's challenges.

Prayer allows you to rely on God. Prayer will enable God to work on your behalf and intervene in your situation. Prayer is how you access what has already been provided by God. You are not getting God to do something new. You are receiving what God has already done. The temptation is to think, "Why pray to God about my situation or issues? He already knows." But you must permit Him to work in your life. For example, in Philippians 4:6–7, God promised peace beyond what you can understand. However, prayer is the vehicle that delivers that peace, making you feel calm and centered amidst life's storms.

When you go to God in prayer, don't just pray about the problem. Pray for the promises of God to manifest in your life. If you need peace, you want to pray and remind God of His Word.

That means you're not solely telling Him everything wrong, what people are doing, and how bad it's making you feel. There is no faith in that. Instead of focusing on the problem, focus on the promise. When you pray a prayer of faith, there is a confident expectation that God will change your situation, so you pray according to what the Word of God tells you can be your reality. The Bible says that the prayer of faith will save the sick (James 5:15). It also says if we ask anything according to His will, He hears us (1 John 5:14). To experience victory in your life, you must believe by faith that the Lord heard what you have prayed, and it is already done.

Your life may be full of pressures–schoolwork, relationships, family expectations, and the uncertainty of the future. It's easy to feel like you're in over your head, but prayer is your lifeline. It's your connection to the One who is bigger than all your challenges. When you take your worries to God in prayer, you're not just venting your frustrations; you're tapping into divine strength and guidance. You're allowing God to step into your circumstances and bring the change that only He can bring. Make prayer a daily habit, and watch how your faith grows stronger and your peace deepens, even during life's storms.

PRAYER

Lord, I ask You to give me the peace that passes anything that I can understand. You said that I can cast my cares on You because You care for me. I lay at Your feet , Lord, anything that is causing me anxiety. I allow the peace of God to reign in my life today. I will not be overwhelmed with fear, worry, and negativity. I thank You for Your blessings, Your love, and Your strength at work in me today! In Jesus' name, amen.

REFLECT

What areas in your life do you need the peace of God? As you identify these areas: First, remember what God has promised you; second, pray and ask God for help; and third, thank Him for His goodness and mercy.

In the same way, faith by itself, if it is not accompanied by action, is dead.

James 2:17

DAY 7

FAITH IN ACTION

In the last devotional entry, I wrote about the power of prayer. Prayer is a critical step to exercising our faith in God. However, after we pray, we must choose to participate in following God's instructions. We must follow His leading. Our decision to obey God is a significant way to know we trust God. We have a level of responsibility in each situation we face. We are responsible for obeying God, doing what we know to be right, and trusting God with the results.

The verse for today highlights the importance of acting on God's instructions, reminding us that faith without action is dead. As you read the Bible, you will notice that every time you see someone using their faith and trusting God, they had to decide to do or say something that allowed them to participate with God. This often happened before they saw the manifestation of what God promised. This stress on the importance of obedience in faith should make you feel committed and dedicated in your journey of faith.

For example, you might be sitting on a chair while reading this. If you're not, you can picture the last time you sat in a chair. You probably sat down in it with no problems or complications. You likely didn't examine the chair first to determine its capability to hold you. You just sat without a second thought. Why is that? Because you believed that the chair could successfully hold your weight. And because you believed that, your actions confirmed your belief. In short, you behaved like you believed it. Behavior is always an indicator of what we believe. When we have faith in God, our actions will show it.

Most people don't know I have a health and exercise science degree. Many years ago, I was a personal trainer. People would hire me to help them reach their health and fitness goals. It would be foolish for someone to tell me their health goals and think they will achieve them without putting in the hard work of a healthy diet and regular exercise. Their participation is vital if they want to have better health. The same is true with our faith. We can only experience the victory that faith in God brings if we decide to partner with God, saying yes to His direction and instruction.

If you are in a situation where you are asking God for better friends, He might lead you to start a conversation with someone you never would have approached before. If you are believing God for a job, a new pair of shoes, or a car, He may lead you to give some money or something valuable to someone else in need as a seed. (We will discuss this more in a later devotion.) If you ask God to help you get better grades, He may prompt you to rearrange your daily schedule, put away social media, and set aside more time to study. In every case, God will ask you to participate in His plan, which allows you to see the manifestation of what you believe. As you step out in faith, trusting God, get ready to do what He leads you to do. You will experience a victory before your very eyes!

PRAYER

Lord, I ask You to help me to be sensitive to Your leading and Your instruction. I ask for boldness to do what faith requires. I will step up with courage every time I step out in faith. I commit to put action to my faith and not be lazy. I know that You will lead me in the paths of righteousness. Regardless of what the situation looks like, I will follow You wholeheartedly. In Jesus' name, amen.

REFLECT

What steps do you feel like God is leading you to take in the areas where you are trusting Him? What are some of the obstacles that might prevent you from following God's instructions?

WEEK 2
GROWING DEEPER IN FAITH

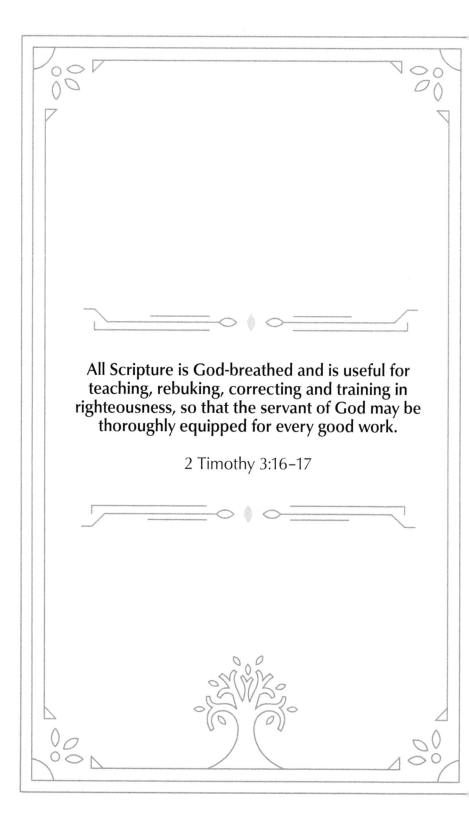

All Scripture is God-breathed and is useful for teaching, rebuking, correcting and training in righteousness, so that the servant of God may be thoroughly equipped for every good work.

2 Timothy 3:16–17

DAY 8

SCRIPTURES ARE THE ANCHOR TO YOUR FAITH

When I was first learning to drive a car, I remember consistently reminding myself to put the car in park when I was done driving. One time, I forgot to put the car in park, and the vehicle almost rolled into the car in front of me. Oops! Thank God I was able to hit the brake in enough time to avoid an accident.

When I think of an anchor for a boat, it's like a car being placed in park. That anchor holds the ship in place so it won't float away or hit something else, causing damage. For us as believers, the Scriptures are the anchor of our faith. They provide us with something concrete that we can believe. They give us a profound sense of security and comfort, assuring us that we won't drift away or cause harm. Without the Word of God, we have nothing for our faith to grab onto. The Scripture says that faith comes by hearing and hearing by the Word of God (Romans 10:17). Without the Word of God, we have no foundation for our faith. The Bible also says that this hope we have is an anchor for the soul, firm and secure (Hebrews 6:19).

In an earlier devotion, I mentioned that faith is believing that God is who He said He is, He will do what He said He would do, and He will do it for you. That statement has three parts that we can connect back to the Bible.

1. The Word of God is essential for our faith because it first teaches us about God—His character and nature. We learn who God is and that He can be trusted.

2. The Word of God teaches us about His promises for us and what He has done and prepared for us.

The stories of the Bible repeatedly show that God will do what He said He would do according to His promises.

3. The Word of God shows us how His promises apply not only to the people in the Bible but also to us today. God is still doing miracles today if we believe. As Jesus says, all things are possible to him who believes (Mark 9:23).

For example, you may need healing in your body. First Peter 2:24 gives you the promise of divine healing, "He himself bore our sins in his body on the cross…'by his wounds you have been healed.'" This is the promise of God, in His Word, that you can now anchor your faith to. It's not just a promise, but a powerful transformation waiting to happen. You can attach your expectation to this Scripture and believe that God will heal your body of sickness, pain, or disease.

God's Word is the instruction manual He's given to teach us how to live as believers. It's not just a book of ancient wisdom; it's a living guide that is relevant to every aspect of our lives. It teaches, corrects, and trains us how to live a life that is both dependent on God and pleasing to Him. When you don't know what to do, the Bible has an answer that can be applied to every situation. I encourage you to read your Bible daily. It equips you with what you need to win in life, providing guidance and support in every step of your journey!

PRAYER

Lord, I choose to let Your holy Scriptures be the anchor to my faith. I will be a hearer and a doer of the Word of God. Your Word is the final authority in my life. I ask that You illuminate my darkness and give me proper understanding of Your Word. Teach me Your Word, Lord, so that I may walk in Your truth. Give me a deeper hunger for Your Word, that it may prosper me in everything I do. I will believe You! In Jesus' name, amen.

REFLECT

Find three scriptures that really resonate with you and make a goal to memorize them over the next thirty days. Write those scriptures down below.

_____

_____

_____

_____

_____

_____

_____

_____

_____

_____

_____

_____

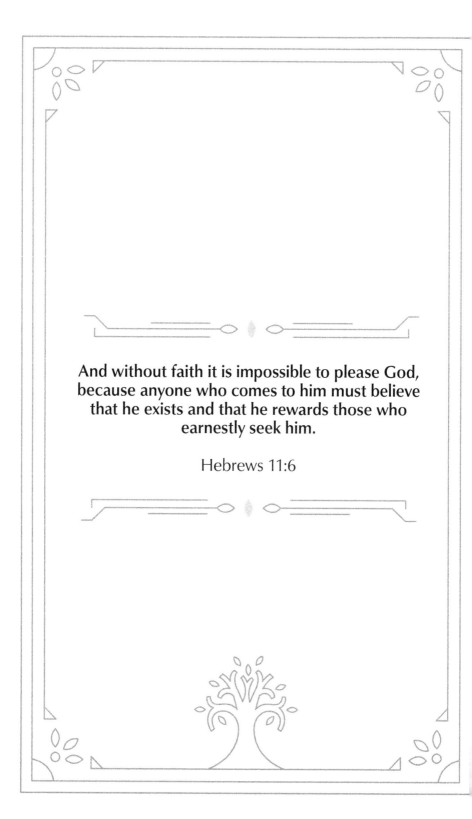

And without faith it is impossible to please God, because anyone who comes to him must believe that he exists and that he rewards those who earnestly seek him.

Hebrews 11:6

DAY 9

FAITH IS HOW YOU PLEASE GOD

Have you ever wondered what it means to please God? It's a big question, but the Bible tells us that faith is a huge part of it. In fact, the Book of Hebrews says that it's impossible to please God without faith. Faith is trust in God. He is pleased when we trust Him and look to Him for direction, provision, healing, strength, and anything else we might need in life. For instance, when faced with a difficult decision, we can trust God's wisdom and seek His guidance through prayer and scripture. When we are in need, we can trust God's provision and believe that He will meet our needs according to His riches in glory (Philippians 4:19).

When we trust God, we make Him the focal point of our expectations. We put Him in His rightful place as the head of our lives, and this is precisely where God wants to be. When He was giving the Ten Commandments to Moses (in addition to more than six hundred other laws) in the Book of Exodus, we see that the very first commandment He gives Moses is this: "You shall have no other gods before me"(Exodus 20:3).

In today's culture, it's less common to worship sculpted images than they did in ancient Egypt. But we have things like social media, money and goods, artists and entertainers, relationships, trends, etc., all fighting for our attention. Sometimes you can be tempted to look to those things as a source of direction, strength, or comfort. However, God wants to be the source of those things for you. When you place your confidence in Him first, He is pleased because you have acknowledged His sovereignty in your life.

God is also pleased when you listen to His direction and obey it. Many times the Bible mentions how God was displeased when His people did not obey Him. This lack of obedience often indicates a lack of trust. Think about it like this: What if you are a part of a mentoring program mentoring another young kid, and you are asked to give them support, encouragement, wisdom, and direction–keeping them on the right path? What if they asked you questions to get your advice on things in their life? They need direction, and you give it to them. Then, the next week you ask them how things turned out, and you find that they didn't take any of your direction. This becomes a pattern that goes on for many weeks. You might feel like you are wasting your time because they don't value what you are offering them. But if they were to follow your advice and see good results every time they did, that would please you.

Similarly, God is pleased when we heed His direction and obey Him. To discern God's direction, we can pray for wisdom, seek advice from mature believers, and compare our decisions with the principles in the Bible. He loves when we follow Him first, not last.

When we choose to trust God, even in the midst of doubts or struggles, it strengthens our relationship with Him. It shows that we believe He is who He says He is and that His promises are true. Think about it this way: trusting a friend with something important strengthens your relationship. It's the same with God. When we trust Him with our lives, dreams, fears, and every-thing else, it deepens our relationship with Him. It shows that we rely on Him more than anything or anyone else. God wants us to have faith because it connects us to Him in a special way. It's not about being perfect or having all the answers. It's about believing in His love and plan for us, even when we can't see what's ahead.

PRAYER

Lord, I will seek to please You every day by trusting in Your plan, provision, and promises for my life. You are sovereign and all Your ways are good. I will step out and believe You even when things are hard. Help me not to trust in the things of the world. I know that when I seek You, I will discover the great things You have for me. In Jesus' name, amen.

REFLECT

Have you ever trusted God and felt that He was pleased with you? How did that make you feel? Why do you think God is pleased when you use your faith?

_____

_____

_____

_____

_____

_____

_____

_____

_____

_____

_____

_____

_____

_____

No temptation has overtaken you except what is common to mankind. And God is faithful; he will not let you be tempted beyond what you can bear. But when you are tempted, he will also provide a way out so that you can endure it.

1 Corinthians 10:13

DAY 10

OVERCOMING TEMPTATIONS BY FAITH

"I can just look at this quickly. No one will know. I'm looking at this on incognito mode, so my web browsing history can't be seen."

"I can just take this. No one will even realize it is gone. And if they do, they won't know it was me."

"Maybe I don't need to tell the truth. Just a little lie will be easier, and there will be less drama."

Temptation is a universal struggle, one that everyone, at some point, has to grapple with. It's not always easy, but with God's help, we can overcome any temptation sent our way. Our faith in God is what can give us the strength to withstand the things that try to tempt our flesh. It's important to know where temptation comes from. The Bible says that God does not tempt anyone, so we are drawn away by our impure desires (James 1:13–16). Satan tries to capitalize on these desires of our flesh and persuade us to do the wrong thing. Then, if we act on desire or temptation, sin is birthed. I had a seminary professor say a statement I have always remembered: Sin is trying to meet a legitimate need, illegitimately. Well said, professor.

Sin often tries to convince us to get something we might need the wrong way. Maybe it's healthy intimacy in relationships, and the enemy may try to convince you that inappropriate sexual activity (pornography, fornication, homosexual activity, etc.) is the way to get it. Or what if you need finances or clothes? The enemy may try to persuade you that taking something that is not yours, shoplifting, or cheating someone out of their money is the way you meet your needs. My friend, that way only ends with harmful consequences. Those, and many others, are suggestions from the enemy that can take you down the path of destruction. We end up hurting ourselves and often hurting others, too. When satan tries to tempt you to do the wrong thing, the Bible says we can get him to flee if we resist him (James 4:7). Every time we resist him, it gets easier.

God's ultimate desire is that we trust Him to meet our needs, both internal and external. The scripture today reminds us of the faithfulness that God shows toward us by making a way out of difficult situations. He will not allow you to be in any situation that you don't have the faith necessary to get you out of. As we ask God to help us escape temptation and trouble, He will show us what to do. Maybe there is a friend that you need to cut off. There may be a place you don't need to go anymore because the environment is negatively affecting you. Or maybe you need to put a lock on your smartphone to keep you from looking at inappropriate things.

Our faith in God will not only allow us to identify what we need to do to escape temptation, but it will also remind us that God can provide whatever we feel we are missing. When you say no to temptation, you are deciding to say yes to God. You are making a declaration that His way is better than what this world has to offer.

PRAYER

Lord, help me overcome the temptations that I'm facing in my life. Help me to see the way out that You have made for me. Give me wisdom and strength to make the right adjustments and decisions, even when it's hard. You are the one I will look to for all of my needs. I know You are there for me, even when I am tempted. Sin has no power over me. Help me to surround myself with the right people, influences, and environments that would be pleasing to You. In Jesus' name, amen.

REFLECT

What are some temptations that you have felt lately? How are you dealing positively with those temptations? Have you ever allowed God to help you overcome a temptation? If so, describe how that made you feel.

Consider it pure joy, my brothers and sisters,
whenever you face trials of many kinds, because
you know that the testing of your faith produces
perseverance. Let perseverance finish its work so
that you may be mature and complete,
not lacking anything.

James 1:2-4

DAY 11

FAITH IN HARD TIMES

Life can be a roller coaster, with many ups and downs that sometimes feel overwhelming. As teenagers and young adults, you're navigating a lot: school pressures, friendships and romantic relationships, family dynamics, and personal challenges. It's easy to feel like you're drowning in everything, but you're not alone, even when it feels like it.

Today's passage, James 1:2–4, offers a perspective that directly relates to the challenges we're facing. It encourages us to find joy in difficult situations, as they cultivate perseverance, leading to our maturity. These trials can be the resistance that strengthens our faith, shaping us into better versions of ourselves.

If you're an athlete doing weight or resistance training to improve your performance, you cannot get stronger, faster, or more powerful without the weight pushing against you. The resistance provides what is necessary for the growth and development of your muscles. Likewise, God will use the resistance that life gives us and supply the faith to push back. I always say that the trials of life aren't meant to slow you down; they are intended to grow you up.

In those challenging moments, when it feels like the world is against you, remember that God is there, ready to walk with you. He's not a distant figure, but your constant companion, rock, and refuge. Psalm 46:1 assures us, "God is our refuge and strength, an ever-present help in trouble." No matter what you face, God is there to strengthen you. Continue to submit to His will.

Often, what you focus on can either help you endure or make you want to quit. Focus on God's promises for you. Faith in hard times means trusting God has a plan, even when you can't see it. It's about believing that His love for you is unwavering, regardless of your circumstances. Romans 8:28 reminds us, "And we know that in all things God works for the good of those who love him, who have been called according to his purpose." Even when life seems chaotic, God is still working behind the scenes for your good. And if what you see isn't good, God is still at work. Let Him cook! A good outcome is on the way. Your faith in God is your strength, empowering you to endure and persevere.

Remember, faith is like a muscle—it grows stronger when it's tested. When you face difficulties, view them as opportunities to exercise your faith. Lean into God's promises, speak His Word over your life, and trust that He is with you every step of the way. You're not just enduring these trials; you're growing through them, becoming the person God created you to be. Keep your eyes on Him, and let your faith lead you to the victory that's already yours in Christ.

PRAYER

Lord, help me to focus on You even in the hard times. Allow me to see what You are doing even in my difficult situations. Help me to have a joyful attitude. Because You are the Lord of my life, I know that anything I will face will work out for my good. Help me to grow in character, perseverance, and love as I face the challenges of life. I will see a new level of maturity as a result of whatever I face. I trust You, Lord. In Jesus' name, amen.

REFLECT

What are some tough things that you are going through this week? How do you think God can use those challenges to make you better? List three to five ways that challenges can make you better.

Be kind and compassionate to one another,
forgiving each other, just as in Christ God
forgave you.

Ephesians 4:32

DAY 12

FAITH AND FORGIVENESS

Forgiving others can be one of the most challenging and lonely journeys you will face in life. As a young person, you might encounter situations when friends betray your trust, classmates spread rumors, a parent doesn't keep their promises, family members hurt you deeply, or possibly something much more harmful. These experiences can leave scars that make forgiveness seem almost impossible. But as followers of Christ, forgiveness is not just a suggestion; it's a commandment and a path to freedom.

Choosing to forgive doesn't mean forgetting or excusing the hurtful actions of others. It's a decision to release the grip of bitterness and anger from our hearts. Today's scripture encourages us to do just that. Jesus taught us about forgiveness through His life and words. In Matthew 6:14–15, He says, "For if you forgive other people when they sin against you, your heavenly Father will also forgive you. But if you do not forgive others their sins, your Father will not forgive your sins." Forgiveness is not just about letting go of resentment; it's about recognizing that God has forgiven us of so much.

When Jesus was teaching the disciples to pray, part of that prayer was, "Forgive us our sins, for we also forgive everyone who is indebted to us" (Luke 11:4, NKJV). I like to think about forgiveness like this: When someone has wronged you, a debt must be paid. You can either make them pay for it through revenge, suffering, withdrawal of intimacy (aka ghosting), etc. Or you pay the debt they created through the suffering of your own. That "suffering" is called forgiveness. That's why it feels so hard sometimes. You are paying off a debt that you didn't create. It's like if someone stole your credit card and went on a shopping spree, and then you agreed to pay the charges, even though you did not create the debt. It's right for them to pay for what they did, but you decide to settle it and pay for it anyway. You gave them something that they didn't deserve: forgiveness.

So how do we do this even when our emotions are all over the place? We forgive by faith. Jesus instructed His disciples to do this when they were met with His challenge to forgive (Luke 17:1-6). He showed them that the key is to speak to the situation. With forgiveness, you must say it before you feel it. Forgiving by faith means trusting in God's love and declaring your confidence in Him to help you exercise compassion. It's choosing to give them what they may not deserve. It's not about waiting until you feel like forgiving, but about making a conscious decision to forgive, trusting that God will help you follow through. There may not be anything else that makes us more like Christ than when we choose to forgive someone who has wronged us.

Forgiving others doesn't always happen instantly. It's a process that requires prayer and a willingness to surrender your pain to God. You may have to forgive a person every day for weeks until that forgiveness has taken root in your heart. In those moments when you struggle to forgive, you can turn to Him for strength. Through His grace, He will empower you to extend forgiveness even when it feels impossible on your own. One practical tip is to pray for the person you need to forgive. This can help soften your heart and change your perspective. Another tip is to remind yourself of the times when you have been forgiven and how it felt. This can help you empathize with the person who has wronged you and make it easier to forgive. Forgiveness is often not easy, but when you do it by faith, God will help you through it.

PRAYER

Lord, help me to forgive _____ for what they did. Even though what they did hurt me, I ask for Your strength to help me release them of this debt. I choose to walk in love. As I forgive them, I thank You for healing my heart from any pain this has caused. Today, I pray that You bless _____ and watch over them. In Jesus' name, amen.

REFLECT

Who do you need to forgive and why? What are some things that make forgiveness so difficult? Have you ever had to forgive someone for something very difficult? How did you feel afterward?

_____

_____

_____

_____

_____

_____

_____

_____

_____

_____

_____

_____

And let us consider how we may spur one another on toward love and good deeds, not giving up meeting together, as some are in the habit of doing, but encouraging one another —and all the more as you see the Day approaching.

Hebrews 10:24-25

DAY 13

FAITH FOR THE RIGHT FRIENDS

Friendships can significantly impact our lives. Good friends can give us the encouragement we need when times are tough and the stability we need when life is changing. Bad friends can do the opposite, pulling you down when you are trying to move forward and bringing unwanted drama into your life. There is no doubt that God made us for relationships. But it can be hard to live a life that honors God with the wrong friends.

God designed us for community, where friendships can flourish and faith can grow stronger together. The Bible tells us to motivate one another to acts of love and good works. Proverbs 27:17 says, "As iron sharpens iron, so one person sharpens another." This means that the friends you choose can influence your life deeply. Surrounding yourself with friends who share your Christian values and encourage your walk with God is vital. They can lift you up when you're down, pray with you when you're struggling, and celebrate your victories with you.

In a world where peer pressure and trends can pull you in all different directions, having friends who stand firm in their faith can provide a solid footing. They'll remind you of God's truth when you're tempted to compromise, and they'll encourage you to stay strong in your convictions. They can also be a source of truth and a sobering reminder of your Christian values if you find yourself going down the wrong path or hanging with the wrong crowd.

Being part of a Christian community also means being a friend who cares deeply for others. The Bible encourages us to carry one another's burdens (Galatians 6:2). When you support and show love to others in your community or friend group, you reflect the love of Jesus and build a stronger bond with one another. Don't just look for good friends; be a good friend too. It's not just about finding good friends but also about being a quality friend in the good and hard times. This is a responsibility and commitment we all share in a Christian community, and it's crucial for the health and growth of our faith and relationships.

If you don't have any friends like I've mentioned, I have good news for you! God can and will give you better friends–if you trust Him with your friendships. How do you do that? Disconnect from the people He's telling you to cut off. That simple act of obedience shows God that you trust Him in this area. And it also makes room in your life for who's next. I've personally seen this work with teens for many years. God never disappoints, even with your squad. Trust that God will supply all of your needs in life, including good friends, and you'll be happy you did. This principle doesn't just apply to friendships but can apply to romantic relationships as well. The transformative power of God's provision of good relationships is something to look forward to. It's a source of reassurance and hope, knowing that God is always working for your good. Together, you can impact the world for Christ.

PRAYER
Lord, I make a decision to trust You with my friendships and every relationship I have. I know You have a good plan for me. Help me disconnect from any friends that shouldn't be in my life or are causing me harm. Help me to be open to new people and friendships. I declare that all of my relationships will glorify You. I commit to being a good loving friend that honors You and encourages others to do the right thing. In Jesus' name, amen.

REFLECT

Do you have some friends that you need to let go of? What has stopped you from disconnecting with them? Describe what a "good friend" means to you. Are you being that kind of friend to others?

He replied, "Because you have so little faith. Truly I tell you, if you have faith as small as a mustard seed, you can say to this mountain, 'Move from here to there,' and it will move. Nothing will be impossible for you."

Matthew 17:20

DAY 14

FAITH THAT MOVES MOUNTAINS

Have you ever wondered what it means to have faith that moves mountains? Sounds impossible, right? Well, that's precisely the point. We serve a God who can do impossible things. When we place our faith in God, we can expect to see the miraculous. Having faith that moves mountains isn't about physical mountains; it's about the challenges and obstacles we face in life that seem impossible to change. It's about trusting God wholeheartedly, even when things seem impossible. There might be times when you encounter mountains of doubt, fear, peer pressure, uncertainty about the future, or insecurity about your capabilities. If you stay in faith, God will help you experience victory through these obstacles.

Jesus doesn't demand flawless faith. He assures us that even faith as small as a mustard seed—seemingly insignificant—can unleash God's power in miraculous ways. When you entrust God with that mustard seed–sized faith, He can work wonders in and through you. Whether it's receiving bad news from a doctor's report, being bullied at school or on social media, facing money shortages, or experiencing problems with family members, faith is the answer. With faith, you are never out of options.

One day, a guest speaker from Nigeria shared a remarkable testimony at our church. A family member of a woman on staff at their church was kidnapped. The kidnappers took her to a remote area where she had no idea where she was. She was in the midst of the forest, sitting on the ground, scared, not knowing what to do. She bowed her head and decided to exercise her trust in God by singing a praise song that she learned at church:

"You are always there to help me, even when no one else is there. I'll still have faith in Your Word that You are always there for me." She just kept singing it over and over.

Finally, when she finished singing, she opened her eyes, lifted her head, and was shocked to discover that she was right on the highway next to a military checkpoint. But what's incredible is she had not physically moved her body nor was she in a vehicle. The last thing she knew was she was sitting on the ground in the forest. So what happened? She had been spiritually transported to safety, just like Elijah in the Bible (2 Kings 2:11). It sounds like something from a Marvel movie, right? I've heard other testimonies similar to this where God supernaturally transported someone.

Remember, my friend, nothing is impossible with God. With faith, all things are possible. When you face challenges, don't underestimate the power of prayer. Pray boldly, asking God for wisdom and strength, and expect to see a miracle. I've witnessed people healed of terminal sicknesses and crippling conditions. I've seen gold teeth appear in people's mouths and the blind regain their sight. I've even seen people pronounced dead come back to life. I've seen families that were broken beyond repair be reconciled back together again. These are not isolated incidents but manifestations of God's power in response to fervent prayer. There are no impossible situations with God. He is with you, ready to move mountains in your life as you trust in Him and pray without ceasing.

PRAYER

Lord, help me to exercise my faith even in the areas where I think it seems impossible. Nothing is impossible for You. I will speak to the mountains in my life and command them to move by Your mighty hand. I will stand firm in believing. I command fear and doubt to leave now! I know that You are a miracle-working God, and You are working miracles in my life. You have given me the victory! In Jesus' name, amen.

REFLECT

What are some situations that you (or your family) are facing that seem impossible? Have you ever seen or heard about God doing a miracle? Have you ever experienced one in your own life? If so, what was it?

_____

_____

_____

_____

_____

_____

_____

_____

_____

_____

_____

WEEK 3

LIVING OUT FAITH

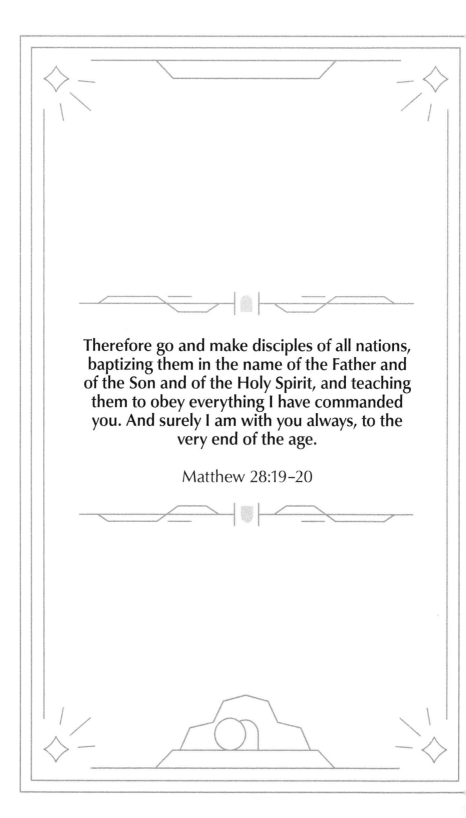

Therefore go and make disciples of all nations, baptizing them in the name of the Father and of the Son and of the Holy Spirit, and teaching them to obey everything I have commanded you. And surely I am with you always, to the very end of the age.

Matthew 28:19–20

DAY 15

SHARING YOUR FAITH

Sharing your faith is one of the most exciting and fulfilling parts of being a follower of Jesus. Before Jesus ascended into heaven after being crucified and resurrected, He gave some simple instructions to His disciples. Today's verse is called the Great Commission, and Jesus is instructing His disciples to make more disciples and teach these new disciples everything that He taught them. Even though this was spoken to the disciples two thousand years ago, it still applies today to us. This Great Commission isn't just for pastors or missionaries; it's for all believers, including you!

I like to remind people that it's called the Great Commission, not the "Great Option." Jesus' instruction is not optional. Sharing your faith means telling others about the love of Jesus and inviting them into a personal relationship with Him. It's about living out your faith in a way that others can see and asking God for opportunities to share His love with those around you. I always tell students that God wants to use their lives as a walking advertisement for His goodness.

Sometimes, talking about your faith can feel intimidating or uncomfortable. But remember, God equips and empowers you for this mission. Acts 1:8 assures us, "But you will receive power when the Holy Spirit comes on you; and you will be my witnesses in Jerusalem, and in all Judea and Samaria, and to the ends of the earth." The Holy Spirit gives you the courage and words to share Jesus with others. The Holy Spirit is your constant companion, empowering you and giving you access to the power of God that can be displayed through you, letting others know that God is real. Also, sharing Jesus with others encourages other believers to be outspoken about their faith.

Sharing your faith isn't just about words; it's also about actions. Your kindness, compassion, and love for others can speak volumes about the difference Jesus makes in your life. Your trust in God in times of uncertainty, when others may be fearful, will often get the attention of those around you. People are always watching, especially when you're facing challenges or going through tough situations. How you respond–whether with patience, grace, or unwavering faith–can be a powerful testimony of God's work in your life. Actions often speak louder than words, and when your actions reflect the character of Christ, you're showing the world what it truly means to follow Him. You have the power to influence others through your actions.

When you forgive someone who's wronged you, help a friend in need, or stand up for what's right, you display the character of Christ. It's in those everyday moments, the small acts of kindness and the choices you make, that others see the reality of your faith. Even when you're unaware, your actions are a witness to those around you. So, live in a way that honors God, letting your life be the light that draws others to Him. For instance, you can volunteer at a local charity, help a neighbor in need, or be a good listener to a friend going through a tough time.

As you go about your day, look for opportunities to share your faith through your words and actions. It could be inviting a friend to youth ministry service, praying with someone who's struggling, or simply sharing a testimony of how Jesus has changed your life. When you share your faith, you're joining God's mission to bring hope and salvation to the world. Embrace this calling with courage and joy, knowing that God is with you every step of the way.

PRAYER

Lord, I want to live in a way that honors You. Help me to be a light to those around me. Let them see the light of Christ in my life. Give me opportunities to share Your love and truth with those around me. Fill my mouth with the right words to say. Help me, Lord, to be bold about my faith even when it's difficult! In Jesus' name, amen.

REFLECT

List three to five people in your life that you would like to see receive salvation. Take a few minutes this week to pray for them. Pray that they would get the opportunity to hear the gospel and their heart would be open to receive.

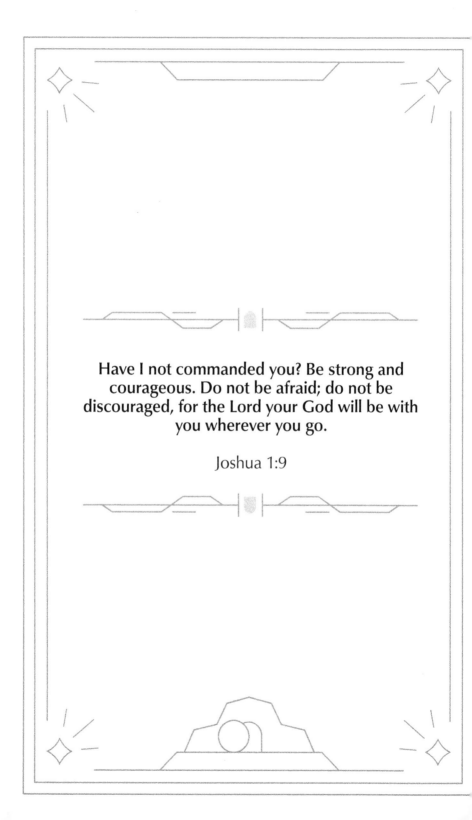

Have I not commanded you? Be strong and courageous. Do not be afraid; do not be discouraged, for the Lord your God will be with you wherever you go.

Joshua 1:9

DAY 16

OVERCOMING FEAR BY FAITH

Everyone has experienced fear—whether it's fear of failure, fear of rejection, fear of danger, or fear of the unknown. Some even develop fears that produce more extreme responses called phobias. Often, these fears are not based on something logical but on a perception of what could happen. For example, a common phobia is the fear of heights. At times, phobias can be the result of past traumas a person has suffered. I like the common acronym False Evidence Appearing Real to understand fear. Satan will often use fear as a way to control people, presenting a mental picture of harm that could come to them if they engage in certain behaviors or conditions. In reality, fear is really just a liar.

As believers, we are not at the mercy of fear. We don't have to let fear control us. Joshua 1:9 reassures us that God commands us to be strong and courageous. Why? Because He is with us wherever we go. We must firmly believe that God's presence is a shield more powerful than any fear. We must have unwavering faith in His protection, provision, and power, knowing that He is always by our side, ready to guide and guard us.

In the Scripture, Joshua faced a massive challenge. He was stepping into Moses' shoes to lead the Israelites into the Promised Land and defeat the giants in Canaan, a daunting task filled with uncertainties. Yet, God's message to Joshua is clear: "Be strong and courageous. Do not be afraid." This wasn't just a suggestion, but a command backed by God's promise of His constant presence.

Psalm 46:1 says, "God is our refuge and strength, an ever-present help in trouble." This promise of God's unwavering presence is a powerful antidote to fear, providing us with the strength and courage we need to face any challenge.

Furthermore, God promises that when fear comes knocking at our door, He will equip us with His power, His love, and the ability to discipline our thoughts so that anxiety is turned into peace (2 Timothy 1:7). You can pray against any spirit of fear and command it to go in the name of Jesus, and it must leave.

So, how can you apply this to your life? First, remember that God's presence is your most significant source of strength. When you're afraid, remind yourself that the Creator of the universe is by your side. He makes the impossible possible. God's ability to protect you is more potent than satan's ability to hurt you, stop you, or make you fail. This truth can transform your fear into faith.

Second, take practical steps of faith. Facing fears doesn't always mean they disappear instantly, but it means trusting God through them. Pray when you're in an anxious situation. Lean into God's promises and take action, even when you're scared. It can also be helpful to cut off any sources that might be feeding fears, such as media, certain information, or peers.

Third, surround yourself with a supportive community. Friends, youth leaders or pastors, and mentors who share your faith can provide encouragement, remind you of God's truth, and pray with you. Their presence can be a source of strength and comfort, reinforcing your faith and helping you overcome fear.

With faith in God, you can face any challenge courageously. Keep God's command to be strong and courageous close to your heart, and trust that He is with you every step of the way.

PRAYER

Lord, thank You for making me strong and courageous. Your Word says that You will never leave me nor forsake me. I will not fear because You are with me. I rebuke any spirit of fear trying to operate in my life or bombard my mind with anxious thoughts. I will take no anxious thought. I thank You, Lord, for keeping me in perfect peace. In Jesus' name, amen.

REFLECT

What fears are you facing right now that you need God's help with? Find a scripture in the Bible that can help you anchor your faith and overcome each fear. Identify someone and have them pray with you about overcoming those fears.

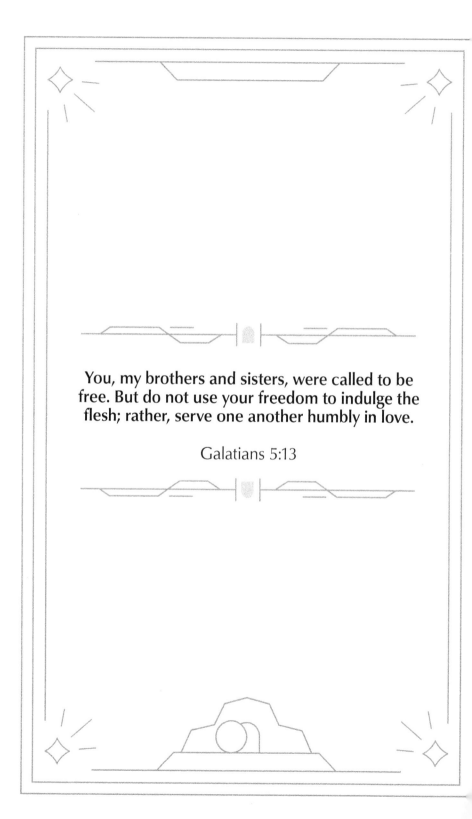

You, my brothers and sisters, were called to be free. But do not use your freedom to indulge the flesh; rather, serve one another humbly in love.

Galatians 5:13

DAY 17

FAITHFUL IN SERVING OTHERS

Have you ever thought about what true freedom means? As Christians, we often talk about the freedom we have in Christ–freedom from sin and freedom to live a new life. But today's scripture tells us something special about this freedom. It says we shouldn't use our freedom to sin or please ourselves but serve others with love.

Serving others is a powerful expression of our faith. When we serve, we reflect Jesus' heart, who came "not to be served, but to serve" (Mark 10:45). This act of service is not merely about doing good deeds; it's about embodying the love of Christ in our everyday actions. Serving others helps us participate in the mission God has given us here on earth while becoming more like Jesus every time we do. Serving is another way to exercise our trust in God, obeying His direction to help others in need selflessly.

I love the passage in John 13:1-17 when Jesus eats the Last Supper with the disciples. After finishing, He starts washing their feet one by one, much to their surprise. But then He says this powerful statement, "I have set you an example that you should do as I have done for you" (John 13:15). The last thing the Messiah did with them before going to the cross was wash their feet. He could have done many things or asked to be served, but He chose to do something selfless. He gave us a blueprint for how God expects us to live. I say this all the time: a person is not ready to lead if they are not willing to serve.

When we serve, we grow in compassion, empathy, and humility. We begin to see people through God's eyes and understand that everyone is valuable and loved. The beauty of serving is that it doesn't require extraordinary skills or resources. It begins with a willing heart. Ask God to open your eyes to the needs around you and give you the courage to step out in faith and help. Whether through small acts of kindness or more significant commitments, your service can be a beacon of hope in a world that desperately needs it. In a world that often emphasizes individual achievement and success, serving reminds us that we are part of a larger family in Christ, each one of us playing a vital role in God's plan.

Look around you—there are countless ways to serve every day. It could be as simple as helping your sibling with their homework, volunteering for a community project, serving at your church, doing yard work for an elderly neighbor, or just being a good listener to a friend. Ask God to show you opportunities to serve and watch Him work through you to bring joy to others and yourself.

Remember, serving others is more than just a one-time action; it's a lifestyle. It's about consistently looking for ways to make a positive impact on those around you. When you serve with a heart full of love, you're not only meeting physical or emotional needs but also planting seeds of faith in the lives of others. As you continue to grow in your relationship with God, let your service be a natural outflow of His love working through you. This is how you truly live out your freedom in Christ—by serving others with the same love and grace He's shown to you.

PRAYER

Lord, help me to serve others around me selflessly. Help me to focus less on myself and more on the needs of others. Put me in the right places where I can use the gifts and abilities that You have given me to bless others. Help me to grow in compassion, empathy, and humility. I want to be more like Jesus every day. In Jesus' name, amen.

REFLECT

What are some ways that you can serve others around you? List three to five things that God is putting on your heart as ways to serve others in your community.

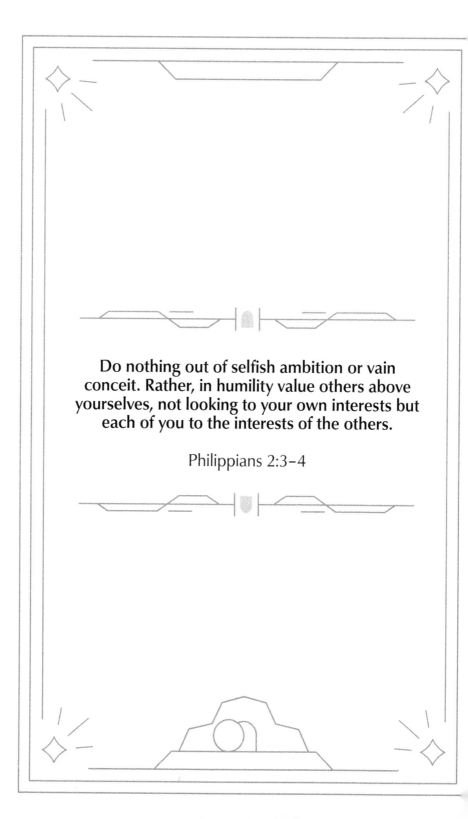

Do nothing out of selfish ambition or vain conceit. Rather, in humility value others above yourselves, not looking to your own interests but each of you to the interests of the others.

Philippians 2:3–4

DAY 18

HUMILITY AND FAITH

Humility might seem countercultural in today's world. Self-promotion is literally everywhere—on social media, in school, and even in sports and activities. It can feel like a constant race to outshine others, with many continually trying to go viral and get someone else to notice or validate them. But the Bible gives us a different perspective. It challenges us to live humbly, putting others before ourselves as a lifestyle.

My wife, Niki, often says that my humility was one of the qualities that initially drew her to me, and continues to do so. It would be far from humble to claim that I'm the most humble person I know, wouldn't it? LOL! But it's true that humility can be appealing to others. After all, who enjoys the company of a know-it-all?

Being humble doesn't mean thinking less of yourself or believing you have nothing to offer. It just means that you think of yourself less. Humility is about recognizing your value in Christ and using your gifts to serve others rather than just promoting yourself. Jesus is the perfect example of this. He had every reason to boast but chose to live a life of humility, ultimately dying on the cross for our sins. He could have started His ministry by announcing, "Hey everyone, I'm HIM! The Messiah has arrived." But He chose to empty Himself of status and allow God's power to work through Him to confirm who He was.

I believe this is what God wants for all of us as His children: to allow His power and love, through our faith in Him, to validate who we are in a world filled with pride and selfish ambition. Humility requires us to trust God. It takes faith to believe that God's way of living—serving others, being selfless, and staying humble–leads to true greatness. When we humble ourselves, we allow God to lift us up in His timing (James 4:10). I like to say, stay humble or you'll stumble. Stay low, and you'll grow. As you stay submitted to God, under His authority and direction, He will help you succeed.

You have unique opportunities to practice humility every day. Maybe it's standing up for someone being bullied or owning up to your mistakes and apologizing when necessary, instead of making excuses or blaming others. It could be sharing responsibilities at home to do chores or showing kindness to someone usually left out. It could be listening to and accepting correction or asking for help when you need it. The list could go on and on. Know that these small acts of humility can make a big difference. Humility doesn't make you weaker; it makes you stronger. Only strong people can be humble.

As you navigate your teenage and young adult years, remember that true humility is a sign of strength, not weakness. The world might tell you to promote yourself, but God calls you to a higher way–one that honors Him and blesses others. Embracing humility isn't about diminishing yourself; it's about making room for God's greatness to shine through you. When you choose to live humbly, you're choosing to live like Jesus, and that's the kind of life that truly makes a difference. So, next time you're tempted to put yourself first, remember the power of humility and trust that God's way will lead you to a life of true significance and impact.

PRAYER

Lord, help me to always be humble and submit to You. I repent if I have operated in pride in any area of my life. Show me how I can exercise humility with my family, friends, classmates, and anyone else that I come in contact with. Help me to be quick to listen and slow to speak. Help me to apologize when I am wrong. I will be an example of Christlike humility to others! In Jesus' name, amen.

REFLECT

What are some good characteristics of humble people? Who do you know that models humility? What are some ways that you can become humbler in your daily life?

You are the light of the world. A town built on a hill cannot be hidden. Neither do people light a lamp and put it under a bowl. Instead they put it on its stand, and it gives light to everyone in the house. In the same way, let your light shine before others, that they may see your good deeds and glorify your Father in heaven.

Matthew 5:14–16

DAY 19

BEING A LIGHT
IN THE DARKNESS

My kids will tell you that in the summertime, especially at night, I always ask them to close the door quickly because bugs will come into the house if they don't. Flying bugs, such as mosquitoes, are attracted to lights. They want to fly right in when they see the lights on in our house through the open doorway. And then I chase them down for the next several minutes like a lunatic and try to kill them because I hate mosquito bites!

The good news is that when you let your light shine, others are attracted to it. This is why Jesus tells us not to hide our light but to let it shine before others. Being the light of the world means living in a way that reflects God's love, truth, and character to everyone around you. You can be a light wherever you are: at school by being kind to the new student, at practice by encouraging your teammates, with friends by speaking words of love and truth, and at home by respecting and loving your family. Your words and actions can make a positive impact and point others to Jesus.

We all have influence. Sociologists tell us that even the most introverted person can influence ten thousand people in their lifetime. The question is, how are you using your influence? Are you using your influence to point others to God? Even on social media, you can decide to be a source of faith, hope, and truth. You can also shine God's light by standing up for what's right and speaking out against injustice. Proverbs 31:8–9 urges us, "Speak up for those who cannot speak for themselves, for the rights of all who are destitute. Speak up and judge fairly; defend the rights of the poor and needy." Your voice can make a difference in bringing hope and justice to those who need it.

Remember, your faith is a powerful tool in influencing others and standing up for what's right, whether in person, in a group chat, or on social media.

As you go about your day, remember that you are called to be a light in this world. God has chosen you to represent Him. Trust Him, knowing that you are the right person for the job. Your belief in God and His promises can spark the interest of others, and the manifestation of God's promises (healing, joy, peace, fulfillment, blessings, etc.) in your life can let others know that God is real. Let your actions and words reflect God's love and truth, and watch as He uses you to make a difference in the lives of those around you. You are a symbol of hope and inspiration, shining God's light in a world that needs it.

And don't underestimate the power of small, consistent actions. Sometimes, simply being kind, forgiving, or standing firm in your beliefs can be the brightest light in someone's life. It's not always about grand gestures; often, it's the everyday choices we make that speak the loudest. When you choose to live out your faith, you're not just a light—you're a beacon guiding others toward the love and grace of God. So go out there, shine brightly, and let the world see the difference Jesus makes in you!

PRAYER

Lord, use me to be a beacon of hope and love to a hurting world. Use my life to inspire others to live a life of faith. Help me not to be ashamed of letting my light shine in front of others. Give me the courage to stand up for what is right even when it is not popular. Use me, Lord, to make a difference wherever I am! In Jesus' name, amen.

REFLECT

What are some ways that you can reflect God's character at school? At home? At practice or when competing against others? How can you use your influence positively on social media?

Truly I tell you, if anyone says to this mountain,
"Go, throw yourself into the sea," and does
not doubt in their heart but believes that what
they say will happen, it will be done for them.
Therefore I tell you, whatever you ask for in
prayer, believe that you have received it, and it
will be yours.

Mark 11:23–24

WEEK 3: LIVING OUT FAITH

DAY 20

FAITH-FILLED WORDS

In a previous devotion, I wrote about faith that moves mountains. Although Jesus mentions another mountain in this scripture, I want to focus on a short three-letter word that makes all the difference when we are using our faith: say.

Words are not just a means of communication; they are incredibly powerful instruments. They can build up or tear down, encourage or discourage, bring life or spread negativity. Proverbs 18:20–21 says, "From the fruit of their mouth a person's stomach is filled; with the harvest of their lips they are satisfied. The tongue has the power of life and death." These words are not just poetic; they carry a weight of responsibility. They are like seeds; when you speak them, you sow them. The harvest of those seeds is the life you experience. What you say can impact not only your life but also the lives of those around you. Your words can determine whether you see the promises of God fulfilled in your life. Your words and prayers either give God permission to work or stop Him from working.

Speaking faith-filled and positive words is not just a practice. It's a powerful tool that starts with believing in God's promises. When you pray, believe that God hears you and is working on your behalf. This belief should extend to how you speak about your life, dreams, and challenges. Instead of saying, "I can't do this," try saying, "With God's help, I can overcome this." Instead of, "I'll never succeed," say, "God has a good plan for my life." Instead of, "I'm always broke," declare, "God, You always give me more than enough." These words are not just a change in vocabulary; they are a transformation of your reality, giving you the ability to bring your life into alignment with God's promises.

WINNING IN LIFE   87

Hebrews 11:3 says, "By faith we understand that the universe was formed at God's command, so that what is seen was not made out of what was visible." It didn't say that the universe came from nothing. It said it came from something not visible–words. Genesis chapter 1 confirms that creation came together at God's command. This means that words have creative power. As we are created in God's image and likeness, He has made us to operate the same way. So, what are you creating with your words?

Consider the impact of your words on your friends and family. Are they filled with encouragement and hope, reflecting your unwavering faith in God's goodness? Develop a habit of speaking life into others. Remember, positive, faith-filled words are not just about being optimistic; they have the power to align your speech with God's truth. When you speak words of faith, you remind yourself and others of God's power and promises, change your mindset, and open your spirit to receive what God has in store for you. Use your words to uplift and inspire, creating a positive and faith-filled environment for yourself and those around you.

Let's take a practical example. If you are experiencing sickness in your body, faith is not about denying the facts, lying about a condition, or pretending that the symptoms don't exist, saying, "I'm not sick." Faith is about declaring, "By Jesus stripes, I am healed." This is how you use your words to speak life. You are not confirming the facts but instead declaring the promises of God. This is how you speak like someone who is winning in life because you have the victory.

This week challenge yourself to speak words that reflect your faith. Start your day with affirmations of God's promises. (See the prayer at the back of this devotional.) Speak positively about your future, trusting that God is in control. Remember, your words have the power to shape your reality. Use them to build a life filled with faith, hope, and love.

PRAYER

Lord, help me to be careful of the words that I speak. Put a bridle on my tongue and a watch over my mouth. I will only say those things that are good, true, positive, and pleasing to You. I will speak blessing and not cursing. Help me, Lord, to honor You with my words. In Jesus' name, amen.

REFLECT

Write down some daily affirmations based on God's promises that you can say daily.

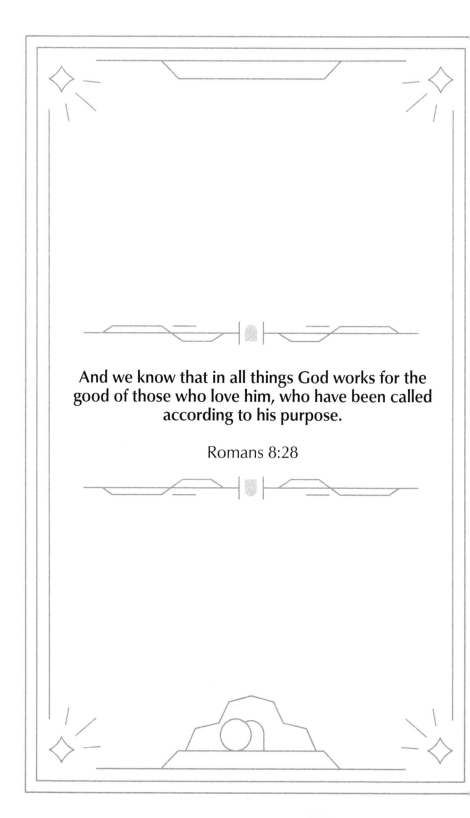

And we know that in all things God works for the good of those who love him, who have been called according to his purpose.

Romans 8:28

DAY 21

COURAGE TO LET GO

Have you ever learned to ride a bicycle? I remember when my parents taught me, and I remember teaching my children how to ride bikes. The scariest part can often be the feeling of being out of control. When you're still learning to coordinate your movements and balance simultaneously, you may be scared that you'll fall and get hurt. No one likes to get hurt. That's probably why we like to be in control—to protect ourselves from what could be painful.

In a world where we're often told to take charge of our lives and plan every detail, it's hard to let go and trust someone else—especially with things that matter most to us. But this verse today gives us a powerful reminder of why giving God control is always worth it; He will make sure that everything always works out for the best for you. It doesn't mean that life will always be easy or go according to our plans, but it means we can trust that God's plan is better than ours. It takes faith and courage to believe this and to let go of our need to control everything.

Giving up control starts with recognizing that we are not alone, and we don't have to handle everything on our own. Psalm 37:23 says, "The Lord directs the steps of the godly. He delights in every detail of their lives" (NLT). This is not a one-time thing, but a continuous process. God is with us, guiding us, and His plans are always for our benefit. When we try to control everything, we're actually limiting what God can do in our lives. It's like holding on to a small piece of our story when God wants to give us a much bigger and better one. His constant guidance and care remind us of His unfailing love when we get cut from a team, fired from a job, denied an application, or dumped by a girlfriend or boyfriend.

Think about the areas in your life where you're holding on too tightly. Maybe it's your grades, future, relationships, or image. It could be family situations or health concerns. What would it look like to surrender these areas to God? It doesn't mean you stop caring or trying; it means you trust God to lead and provide for you. It means you submit to His wisdom and His plan. Victory is not a life without problems. It's a life that faces problems with the promises of God.

So, how do you give up control? Start by praying and asking God to help you trust Him more. When you feel anxious or stressed about something, remind yourself of Romans 8:28 and God's promise to work everything out for good. If you need encouragement, solid Bible-based faith-filled messages can help remind you that God has this, as long as you let Him have control. This is essential because faith comes from hearing the Word of God (Romans 10:17). Prayer and scripture are not just tools; they are weapons that empower you to face life's challenges with faith and courage.

Having the faith and courage to give up control is not easy, but it is incredibly freeing. It allows you to live with peace and confidence, knowing that God always has your back. Trust in His plans and let go, knowing that He is working everything out for your good.

PRAYER

*Lord, forgive me for trying to control things that I shouldn't.
You are the one I will look to for strength, wisdom, and
guidance when things get hard. Help me to have the courage to
face these challenges knowing that You always have my back.
Lord, I will submit to Your plan in every area where I'm tempted
to worry. I cast my cares on You. I trust You, Lord, and I give
You control. In Jesus' name, amen.*

REFLECT

*What are a few areas that you have struggled to give God control?
Is there a situation where you have given God control and His plan
worked out for the best? Describe below.*

_____

_____

_____

_____

_____

_____

_____

_____

_____

_____

_____

WEEK 4

SUSTAINING YOUR FAITH

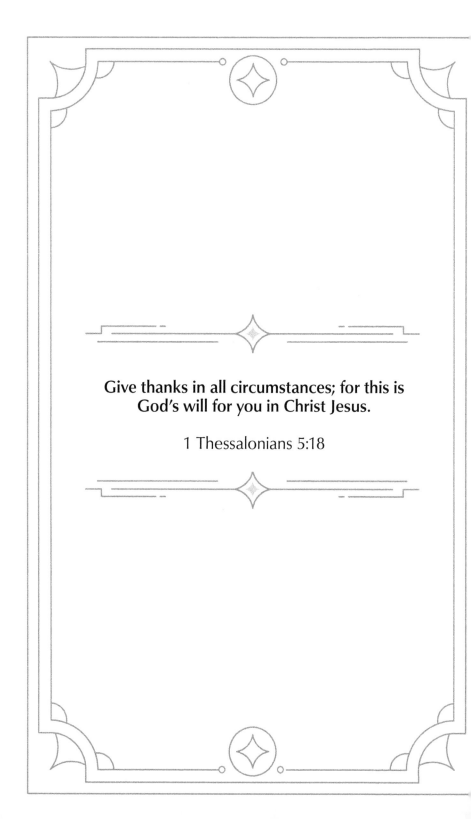

Give thanks in all circumstances; for this is
God's will for you in Christ Jesus.

1 Thessalonians 5:18

DAY 22

DEVELOPING A HEART OF GRATITUDE

There is a saying that the elders always used to state: "Just be grateful for what you have." It's easier now, more than ever, to get caught up in wanting the latest gadgets, the newest iPhone (sorry, Android users LOL), expensive clothes, a larger social media following, or more recognition. Through technology, we have so much exposure to the best of everything. If we are not careful, those things will lure us into having an attitude that is never satisfied with what we have. But when we practice gratitude, we see and appreciate the blessings we already have. It helps us recognize God's goodness in our lives, even in the small things. I like to say, "Never let your wants speak louder than your thanks."

In today's scripture, the apostle Paul reminds us to "give thanks in all circumstances." This might sound easy when things are going well, but it can be challenging when life gets tough. Even as you are holding fast to your faith, believing things will change or you will see a desire fulfilled, you can decide to have a grateful attitude. Developing a heart of gratitude means learning to thank God not just in the good times but in all circumstances. Having an attitude of constant thanksgiving will help you see a better, more godly perspective in every situation.

Gratitude often shifts our focus from what we lack to what we have. When challenges come, gratitude can be a powerful tool. It reminds us of the faithfulness of God. It doesn't mean you should ignore your problems or pretend everything is perfect. Instead, find something to be thankful for, even in difficult times. This might be a lesson learned, a supportive friend, or the strength to overcome a challenging situation. Or you might even find that some situations could have been a lot worse if it wasn't for the grace of God. Gratitude can bring peace and hope, reminding you that God is with you and working for your good. I believe gratitude can remind us to keep trusting God, knowing that victory is sure.

Sharing your gratitude with others can also make a significant impact. Expressing thanks to friends, family, and authority figures (teachers, coaches, mentors, pastors, etc.) shows that you value and appreciate them, which can brighten their day and encourage them to be grateful, too. Developing a heart of gratitude takes practice, but it's worth it. It helps you stay positive, builds your faith, and draws you closer to God.

When you consistently practice gratitude, it affects not only your perspective but also your relationships. You start to see the good in people and circumstances, which can help you build stronger, more meaningful relationships. It also allows you to experience deeper joy and contentment because you're no longer driven by a constant desire for more.

Gratitude becomes a habit that shapes your character, making you more resilient in the face of adversity. Over time you'll find it easier to trust God's plan for your life, knowing that He is always providing for you in ways you might not even realize. As you develop a thankful heart, you'll discover a greater sense of peace and fulfillment, grounded in the confidence that God is in control and His goodness never fails.

PRAYER

Thank You, Lord, for all the blessings that You have given me and my family. Thank You for always watching over me and protecting me. Forgive me for the times I have been selfish or had a bad attitude because things weren't going my way. Help me to be patient in times when I don't get what I want. Allow me to see Your hand in every circumstance. I will give thanks in every situation! In Jesus' name, amen.

REFLECT

Start every day this week by thanking God for at least three things. They don't have to be big—maybe it's good health, a safe place to live, a trustworthy friend, access to education, or a hot meal. By doing this, you train your mind to look for the positive and acknowledge God's blessings in your life.

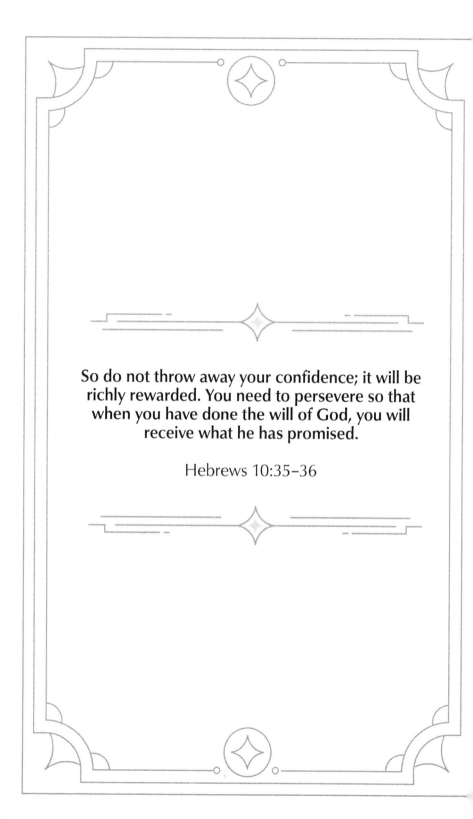

So do not throw away your confidence; it will be richly rewarded. You need to persevere so that when you have done the will of God, you will receive what he has promised.

Hebrews 10:35–36

DAY 23

PATIENCE AND PERSEVERANCE

"What is taking so long?" That's often what we say to ourselves when we don't understand why we have to wait. Whether it's waiting in line at a fast-food drive-through or waiting on test scores for a final exam, no one really likes waiting. Patience isn't something that usually comes naturally. We need the guidance and support of the Holy Spirit to exercise the fruit of the Spirit, in this case, patience.

This passage in Hebrews 10:35–36 reminds us that we need to be patient and persevere so that after we have done God's will, we will receive His promises. We are encouraged not to throw away our confidence or "give up" on God because our commitment will be richly rewarded. This is a source of strength and hope. That's called walking by faith. Life often throws challenges our way. Whether it's academic pressure, relationship issues, or personal struggles, it can sometimes feel overwhelming. During these times, patience and perseverance become essential. It's easy to get discouraged and want to give up when you can't see good results happening quickly, but God calls us to hold on and trust in His timing and plan.

The Bible tells us that through faith and patience, we will inherit the promises of God (Hebrews 6:12). Consider the example of the Israelites. They wandered in the desert for forty years before reaching the Promised Land. Despite the long journey and numerous setbacks, those who persevered (and obeyed God) eventually experienced God's promise. Their story teaches us the importance of trusting God's process, even when it takes longer than we'd like. Trusting God is about understanding that His timing is perfect, and His plan is always better than ours.

Patience is about trusting that God knows what He's doing. When we practice patience, we align ourselves with God's will, allowing Him to work in our lives in His own time. It's about waiting with a peaceful heart. On the other hand, perseverance is about staying committed to our faith, even when things get tough. It's about pushing through obstacles and remaining steadfast in our beliefs, even when it's hard. It's about not giving up, even when we're tempted to. Both patience and perseverance are essential in our spiritual journey, and they often go hand in hand.

To cultivate patience and perseverance:

1. Start by building a solid foundation in God's Word.

2. Spend time in prayer, asking God for the strength to endure and the patience to wait on His timing. Prayer is key.

3. Trusting God is a byproduct of intimacy with Him. Spend time with Him, acknowledging His presence in your life.

It's always easier to trust someone who is close to you than a stranger because you know that person loves you and wants the best for you. Don't let God be a stranger in your life. As your relationship with Him grows, so will your willingness to trust Him.

Remember, every challenge is an opportunity to grow closer to God. Hebrews 12:1–2 says, "Let us run with perseverance…fixing our eyes on Jesus, the pioneer and perfecter of faith. For the joy set before him he endured the cross." Jesus could endure the overwhelming pain of the cross because He saw us returning to the Father. You can endure what you're going through when you can clearly see what you're going to. A solid mental picture of the hopeful outcome God promised is a way to stay strong in faith. This is how you hang on to win and get the victory even when the battles are long. Trust in His promises, hold on to your confidence, and persevere. In doing so, you will not only grow in your faith but also be richly rewarded by the One who loves you and has great plans for your life.

PRAYER

Lord, I will wait on You even when I am tempted to be impatient. I trust Your plan and Your timing. Your Word never fails. Help me to see Your plan. Give me the strength to endure. Your Word says not to get weary in doing good and at the right time I will reap a good harvest if I don't give up. I will stand strong until I see a victory! In Jesus' name, amen.

REFLECT

On a scale of one to ten, one being the least and ten being the most, how patient are you? What are some areas in life that you need to grow in patience? What are some constructive things that you can do while you wait?

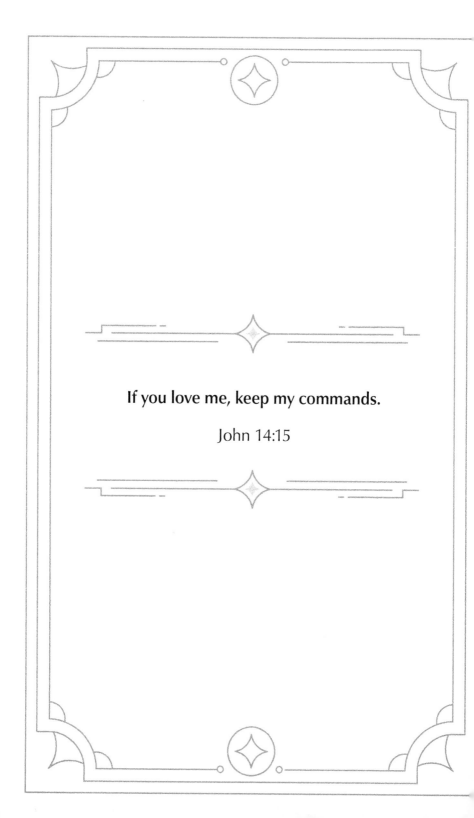

If you love me, keep my commands.

John 14:15

DAY 24

FAITH AND OBEDIENCE

Faith is the very foundation of our relationship with God. It's trusting in His promises, believing in His love, and relying on His strength. But faith without action is incomplete, as I shared earlier. James 2:26 tells us that "faith without deeds is dead." Our actions should always reflect our faith, demonstrating our commitment to following Jesus. True faith isn't just about believing in God; it's also obeying His commands. Today's verse highlights the importance of showing our love for Jesus through obeying His commandments.

Obedience is a practical expression of our faith. Sometimes, God asks you to give something or stop something, or He gives instructions from His Word that might not seem so easy to follow. In those moments, you have to choose that loving God and following Him is the most important thing. I like something my wife says: Faith always manifests itself in obedience.

I remember when I was sixteen and wanted to buy a car. I had a driver's license but didn't have my own transportation. I didn't have nearly enough money to buy a car, but I had some money saved since I worked a part-time job at the church in the facility maintenance department. I asked my dad if he would like to get me a car, and he said, "You can sow a seed for it." Dang it! It was a disappointing answer, but yet something felt right about it. I thought and prayed about it, and ultimately, I felt that it was God speaking through my dad. God was instructing me to "sow a seed" or give an amount of money to Him so He could multiply it and return it back to me. God wanted to make good on His promise in Philippians 4:19, "God will meet all your needs according to the riches of his glory in Christ Jesus."

After Dad and I prayed over this seed, I put my offering in the bucket that Sunday in church. Long story short, weeks later someone gave my dad a sizeable, unexpected amount of money. God then spoke to him and said that what he had received wasn't for him to keep. He was just the vessel. That money belonged to me. It was for my new car. The following week, we bought a brand-new 2002 silver Toyota Camry with cash, no financing, and no payments! My obedience and faith in God prompted God to supply my needs. The same God who did it for me will do it for you if you obey Him.

Obedience is about listening to God's Word and putting it into practice in our daily lives. It's about following His leading. This means making choices that honor God, even when difficult or unpopular. It means showing kindness, telling the truth, stepping out in faith, and standing up for what is right. Faith and obedience can be challenging in a world full of peer pressure and mixed messages. But remember, obedience to God brings blessings and strengthens our faith. When you choose to follow God's commands, you grow closer to Him and become a stronger witness to His faithfulness.

Obedience is not about being perfect; it's about being faithful. The Bible reminds us that Jesus learned obedience through the things He suffered (Hebrews 5:8). Obedience is about striving to do God's will and trusting Him with the results. Let your faith be alive and active through your obedience, and watch how God works in your life.

PRAYER

Lord, I choose to obey You. I love You Father, and I submit to Your will and Your Word. Help me to be sensitive to Your leading. Give me the courage to obey You even when it's hard or inconvenient. Show me how to please You every day, Lord. In Jesus' name, amen.

REFLECT

What are you believing for God to do this week? Have you put actions to your faith? Take five minutes and ask God what the next step is. Write down what you feel God is putting on your heart.

_____

_____

_____

_____

_____

_____

_____

_____

_____

_____

_____

_____

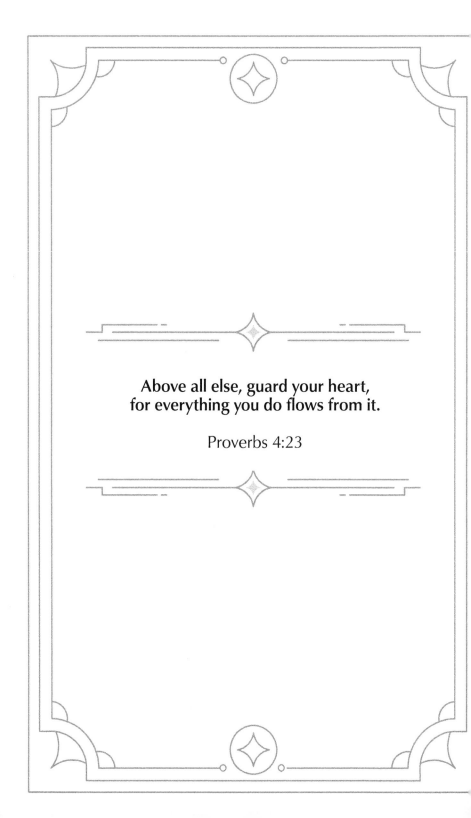

**Above all else, guard your heart,
for everything you do flows from it.**

Proverbs 4:23

DAY 25

GUARDING YOUR HEART AND MIND

I hate weeds. If you've ever had to care for a garden or a yard, you can understand how difficult this can be. I don't know if I've ever seen someone plant weeds on purpose, but they show up almost automatically every spring and summer. For me, most of the work in caring for a lawn or tree bed is directed toward pulling weeds. If I don't pull the weeds, they multiply, and it's only a matter of time before they take over my yard. We should be just as protective—if not more so—with our hearts. Why? Because your heart is like soil, it will grow anything planted in it.

In today's world, we're constantly bombarded with information and influences from social media, friends, school, music, and entertainment. While some can be positive, others can lead us away from God's path. The verse today emphasizes how crucial it is to protect our innermost thoughts and feelings as they influence our actions and decisions. Guarding your heart and mind means being mindful of what you allow into your life and making choices that align with your faith.

I remember a teenage girl asking for prayer after a youth service many years ago. She was so bothered that she was crying. She said that she had been having thoughts of killing her younger brother. I asked if they were fighting. She said no, they have a great relationship. But she couldn't stop the thoughts and voices telling her to do something evil. We prayed together and came against the devil and his attack. Then, I asked what she was putting into her heart. She said that she loved horror movies, which are often filled with lots of violence and murder; she would even fall asleep while they played on the TV at night. This was the root cause of the problem.

Notice that the devil was using media as an open door to sow bad seeds in her heart that were trying to overpower her conscious will. We instructed her to cut that out of her life immediately. I saw her again a few months later, and she was different. She was proud to report that she had no more evil thoughts of murder and was in a much better place. Her story is a testament to guarding your heart and mind. Please remember that just like God wants to influence our thinking, wrong influences can also affect our thinking.

Always be selective about what you watch, listen to, and read. This is not a passive act, but a purposeful choice you make to protect your heart and mind. Choose content that uplifts and encourages you rather than what can lead you astray. Enjoying movies, music, and books is okay, but ensure they align with your values and help you grow in your faith. However, you should diligently guard against things that glorify violence, promote lust (such as pornography), encourage sin or wickedness, and other things that are not pleasing to God. Philippians 4:8 encourages us to think about true, noble, right, pure, lovely, admirable, excellent, and praiseworthy things. Focusing on these qualities helps you develop a heart and mind that reflect God's character. Put good seeds in your heart, meditating on verses in God's Word that remind you of God's love, wisdom, and guidance. You will always reproduce what you meditate.

Prayer is also essential in guarding your heart and mind. Ask God to give you wisdom and discernment to recognize and avoid negative influences. Pray for strength to stand firm in your faith and to make choices that honor Him. Remember, guarding your heart and mind is a daily practice. It requires intention and effort, but the rewards are worth it. Doing this allows God to work in your life and guide your actions. Stay vigilant, stay prayerful, and keep your heart and mind focused on Him.

PRAYER

Lord, help me to diligently guard my heart. Forgive me if I have let anything into my heart that's not pleasing to You. Remove any desire for things that don't glorify You and only feed my carnal nature. I will watch, read, and listen to things that are positive, uplifting, and right. Give me wisdom, Lord, for how to better protect my heart every day. In Jesus' name, amen.

REFLECT

What is something that you are putting in your heart that is not pleasing to God and that you need to cut off?

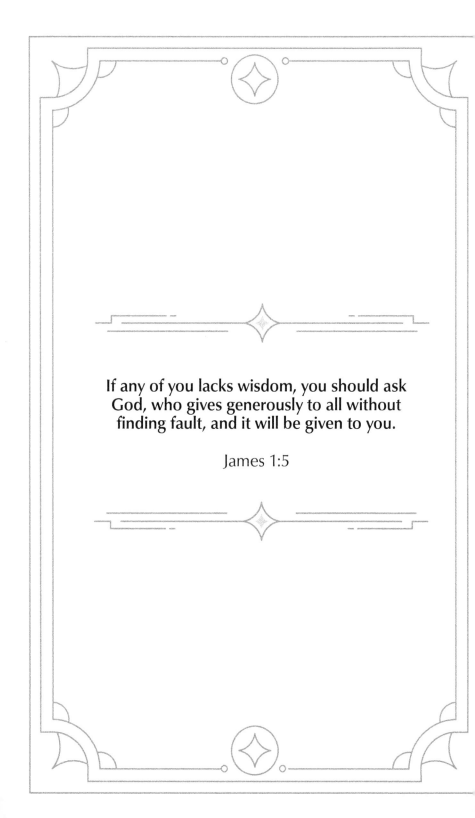

If any of you lacks wisdom, you should ask God, who gives generously to all without finding fault, and it will be given to you.

James 1:5

DAY 26

WISDOM—THE AID TO OUR FAITH

In Genesis chapter 1, you see the creation story and how God spoke creation into manifestation. Through faith in what He spoke, God created all that we see in our natural world. The Bible says in the Book of Proverbs that wisdom was there by God's side, helping Him to form what He had spoken (Proverbs 8:22–30). Wisdom holds a significant relationship to faith. Faith is the *what*, but wisdom provided the *how* this would get accomplished. Wisdom is the divine architect that manifests what faith believes. Wisdom is an essential part of how we can experience victory, which in God's eyes, is living a life that aligns with His will and brings glory to Him.

Life can be full of challenging decisions, from choosing friends to planning your future. (Choosing a college can be a tremendous challenge just by itself.) It's easy to feel overwhelmed and unsure about the right path to take. But James 1:5 offers us an incredible guarantee: if we lack wisdom, we can ask God, and He will generously give it to us without finding fault, helping us in our decision-making process.

First, you may ask, what is God's wisdom? Wisdom is more than just knowledge; it's the ability to make good decisions based on God's truth. In the original translation, the word wisdom means insight or clarity. Godly wisdom allows you to gain a different or deeper perspective on the same situation, changing your understanding and giving you hope. It helps you steer through life's challenges and align your choices with God's will, empowering you to make decisions that honor God.

Seeking God's wisdom starts with faith. We must believe that God is the source of all wisdom and knowledge and that He desires to guide us. Approaching Him confidently is vital because the following verse states, "But when you ask, you must believe and not doubt" (James 1:6). Don't go back and forth, wondering if God will help you. Know that He will.

When you face a difficult decision or need guidance, take it to God in prayer first. Ask Him for wisdom, trusting that He hears you and will respond. This isn't a one-time act but a continual practice of seeking His guidance daily. Reading the Bible is another crucial way to tap into God's divine wisdom. God's Word is full of knowledge and principles that can guide your decisions. Proverbs, in particular, is a treasure trove of practical advice for daily living. As you read, ask God to reveal His wisdom and show you how it applies to your life.

Another way God gives us wisdom is through godly mentors, parents, pastors, and friends who can offer wise counsel. Proverbs 15:22 says, "Plans fail for lack of counsel, but with many advisers they succeed." The wisdom of those who follow God and are mature can help you see situations from a godly perspective. Their insights can be valuable in making decisions that align with God's will.

Seeking God's wisdom is an ongoing journey that requires faith and perseverance. Trust in His timing and remain open to His guidance, even if it comes in unexpected ways. By praying, studying His Word, and seeking counsel, you will gain more understanding, allowing you to make decisions that honor God and lead to winning in life. Trust that God is generous with His wisdom and desires to guide you in every aspect of your life.

PRAYER

Lord, I ask for Your wisdom in every situation that I'm facing. Give me insight, clarity, and understanding that I didn't have before. Help me to know Your will. Through Your wisdom, I will make the right decisions. I thank You for giving me wise counsellors that will offer sound and godly wisdom. I receive it now by faith, in Jesus' name, amen.

REFLECT

What area in your life can you use the wisdom for God? What steps can you take to make wise decisions? Who are some people in your life that you can go to for wise counsel?

_____

_____

_____

_____

_____

_____

_____

_____

_____

_____

_____

_____

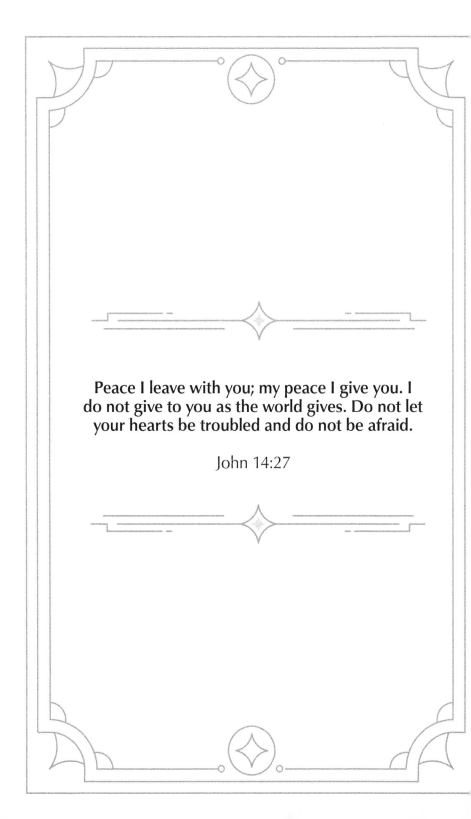

Peace I leave with you; my peace I give you. I do not give to you as the world gives. Do not let your hearts be troubled and do not be afraid.

John 14:27

DAY 27

PEACE IN FAITH

I'm a person who enjoys peace. I like things that promote relaxation, such as soothing sounds and pleasant smells. Laying on the beach in the sun with a nice breeze is a great way to spend a day. But life is not always a sunny day at the beach. It can sometimes be stressful and full of uncertainties. Whether it's school pressures, family issues, work frustrations, or relationship drama, it's easy to feel anxious and overwhelmed. But Jesus offers us a peace that surpasses all understanding and calms our hearts even during chaos, a peace that is even better than that beautiful day at the beach.

In today's verse, Jesus offers a wonderful promise of giving us His peace. This verse reminds us that true peace comes from Jesus, not from the world. Experiencing this peace starts with faith. We must believe that Jesus is with us and that His promises are true. When we trust in His presence and plan for our lives, we can let go of our worries and rest in His peace. Isaiah 26:3 states what I like to call the peace promise, "You will keep in perfect peace those whose minds are steadfast, because they trust in you." God promises to help you find calm in the midst of the chaos if you trust in Him.

I admit it's easier to say this than actually do it. But within this verse lies the secret: focus. Whatever you focus on is what you will get more of. When you focus on the problems, your emotional response only gets amplified. But focusing on God and His plan helps you regulate your emotions, feeling less stressed and anxious about what's going on. The problem may still exist, but because you remind yourself that God is in control and He loves you, your mind will be more at ease. The very foundation of peace is trusting God.

How do we remind ourselves of the peace that Jesus left us? First, we pray. I'm sure you've noticed by now that many things with God start with prayer. Prayer is a powerful way to connect with God and experience His peace. When you're feeling anxious or troubled, take a moment to pray. Share your worries with God and ask Him to fill you with His peace. Philippians 4:6-7 encourages us to present our requests to God, and His peace, which goes beyond all understanding, will guard our hearts and minds in Christ Jesus. You don't have to wait for your problems to end to have peace. You can decide to have peace now.

Another way to fix your focus on God's peace is to immerse yourself in His Word. The Bible is full of promises that can reassure and comfort you. Verses like Psalm 46:10, "Be still, and know that I am God," remind us to pause and trust in God's sovereignty, which means His supreme power and authority over all things. Go to the Bible app and start a seven-day reading plan on the topic of peace. The goal is to flood your thoughts with reminders of His promises.

Worship and music can also be excellent promoters of peace. Singing or listening to worship songs such as "What a Beautiful Name" or "See a Victory" can shift your focus from your problems to God's greatness and love. Listening to worship music is one of my favorite things to do. Because music often connects with us emotionally, it's a way to remind yourself (and your emotions) of who God is and how much He cares for you.

Remember, God's peace is a gift that comes from knowing Him and trusting in His promises. When you place your faith in Jesus and rely on His presence, you can experience a peace that the world cannot give. This peace is not momentary or dependent on circumstances; it's a constant, unwavering presence in our lives.

PRAYER

Lord, I ask for Your peace that passes all understanding today. Help me to focus on Your promises not the problems. I rebuke every anxious thought and declare that everything will turn out for my good. My hope is in You, Jesus, the author and finisher of my faith. In Jesus' name, amen.

REFLECT

Where do you need peace in your life? What are some ways that you've experienced God's peace before? Identify a worship song that can remind you of His peace and presence.

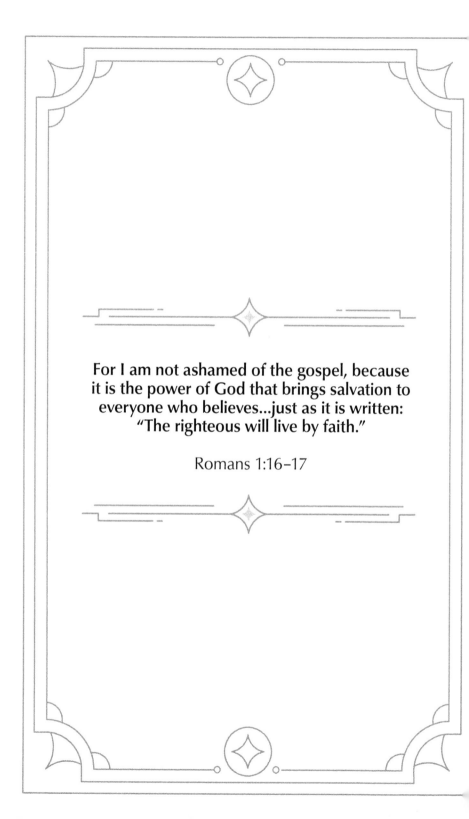

For I am not ashamed of the gospel, because it is the power of God that brings salvation to everyone who believes...just as it is written: "The righteous will live by faith."

Romans 1:16–17

DAY 28

BOLD FAITH

In your generation, it's commonplace to see peers doing TikTok challenges, pulling pranks, and posting on their social media just to boost their following. I must admit that I'm quite surprised sometimes to see the boldness of young people and what they will do for likes and attention. But then I wonder how the generation would be impacted if they took that unashamed audacity and pointed it toward the things of God. Imagine the transformative power if this boldness were directed toward sharing the gospel and how it could shape and influence your generation.

As I've mentioned in an earlier entry, as followers of Christ, we should be committed to sharing the gospel with others. As you continue to exercise your faith in God, it shouldn't be a secret. Your friends and peers should be able to see it because you should be bold about it. These verses in Romans 1 challenge us to be unashamed and courageous in sharing the life-changing message of Jesus with others. Being bold in sharing your faith starts with understanding the power of the gospel, the good news of Jesus Christ–His love, power, sacrifice, and resurrection.

I admit that sometimes sharing your faith can feel intimidating. You might worry about being judged or rejected. But remember, it's not about having all the answers or being perfect. This is where I've seen most young people stall because they feel like their behavior isn't "good enough" to share their faith. They feel like they still have issues they are overcoming, which disqualifies them from sharing the gospel. You might feel like this at times as well.

Your imperfection doesn't nullify the gospel or make it untrue. That is the story of the gospel–imperfect people being perfected because of what a perfect Savior did. It's about being genuine and letting God work through you. Trust that the Holy Spirit will give you the words and the courage you need when you share the gospel. And remember, even if someone doesn't respond positively, it's not a reflection of you or your faith, but a part of their own journey. Keep sharing, and trust that God is using you in ways you may not even realize.

Ask God for opportunities to share your faith boldly this week. Ask Him to open doors and give you boldness. When those moments arise, step out in faith. It could be as simple as sharing a Bible verse that has impacted you, inviting a friend to church or youth group, or telling someone how Jesus has changed your life. For instance, if a friend is going through a tough time, share a comforting Bible verse with them. If you're discussing weekend plans, invite them to your church's youth group. If you're sharing a personal story, mention how your faith has helped you through it. Ask a friend if you can pray for them right there on the spot, not later on. Here's a secret: the more you do it, the easier it gets.

Finally, keep your focus on God's approval, not people's opinions. In Galatians 1:10, Paul writes, "Am I now trying to win the approval of human beings, or of God?" Aim to please God in all you do, including how you share your faith. God's approval is what truly matters, and He is always pleased when you share His love and message. By being bold in sharing your faith, you become a light in the world, guiding others to the hope and love found in Jesus Christ. Embrace the call to be unashamed of the gospel, and watch how God uses you to make a difference wherever you go.

PRAYER

Lord, give me boldness to share the gospel without hesitation. I will live unashamed about my faith in You. Help me to be a positive example to everyone I encounter. Give me courage to stand up for truth, justice, and righteousness. I will be a change agent for the Kingdom of God in my school, community, workplace, family, or wherever I am. In Jesus' name, amen.

REFLECT

Write down three to five ways that you can boldly share the gospel with others that you know. Commit to doing at least one of those things this week.

_____

_____

_____

_____

_____

_____

_____

_____

_____

_____

_____

_____

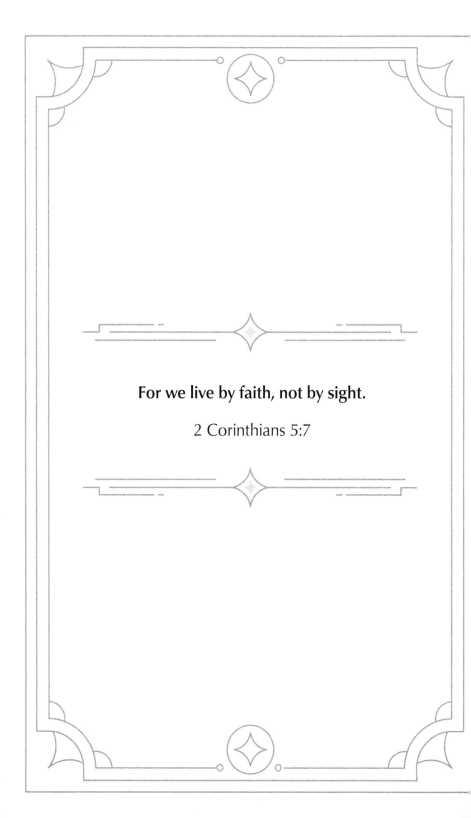

For we live by faith, not by sight.

2 Corinthians 5:7

DAY 29

GROWING YOUR FAITH DAILY

I have to admit, I'm not very good at taking care of plants. It's probably because it's never been very important to me. I forget to water them and prune them. Maybe I need to put them in a better position to get sunlight. I want the plants to live and grow, but I need to do what it takes to make that happen. Just like I want my plants to grow, God wants our faith to grow daily. But to do that, we must do the things that will help it grow. Faith is like a muscle, it needs to be fed, exercised, and put to work to grow strong.

The apostle Paul says something that should be a standard way of living for every Christian believer: we live by faith and not by sight. Faith is not just a one-time thing or something to access in an emergency, like a fire extinguisher in a glass case that reads "break in case of emergency." Trusting in God in times of desperation is indeed the best thing you can do, but God wants you to have faith in Him daily. You can experience God's power and presence in your life every day, even in the small things. God desires for us to grow more and more dependent on Him for His strength, direction, and ability. I love what my dad, Dr. Bill Winston, says, "Faith connects you with God's ability." So my encouragement is this—stay connected to God's ability every day, not just in times of need.

Living by faith means trusting in God and His promises, even when we can't see the full picture. Growing your faith daily is crucial because it not only strengthens your relationship with God and equips you to face life's challenges but also transforms you into someone who reflects His love and truth. It purifies your heart, giving you a desire to live a life that is holy and pleasing to Him. Galatians 2:20 says, "I have been crucified with

Christ and I no longer live, but Christ lives in me. The life I now live in the body, I live by faith in the Son of God, who loved me and gave himself for me." This transformation through faith empowers you to face life's challenges with confidence and grace.

As you depend on God, you will need to spend time with God. Like any relationship, your connection with God deepens through regular communication and time spent together. You build a closer bond with God when you talk to Him about your day, worries, hopes, and desires. This regular communication with God is not just a duty, but a privilege that allows you to feel understood and connected. Reading the Bible helps you understand His character, promises, and will for your life, reassuring you daily that you can trust Him.

As you grow in faith, your actions and decisions will be influenced. You start to live in a way that reflects God's love and truth. Life can be unpredictable and sometimes difficult. Growing your faith daily prepares you to handle whatever comes your way. To grow your faith daily, commit to spending time with God through prayer and Bible study, as I have mentioned multiple times throughout this devotional. Remember, living by faith means trusting God every step of the way. By making faith a daily priority, you'll find strength, peace, and purpose in your walk with God. Winning in life will not just feel like a fantasy; it will become a reality!

PRAYER

Lord, I commit to walking by faith every day. I will depend on Your leading, Your grace, and Your ability. I will look to You for guidance and strength. I will not be led by my feelings, but I will be led by Your Spirit. Help me to continue to grow in Your Word and be strengthened in my spirit. Help me to hear Your voice and follow Your instruction. I will trust You in anything and everything! In Jesus' name, amen.

REFLECT

Set a few faith goals today. How do you want to grow in your relationship with God this year? What are some things that you want God to do in your life or in the lives of your family? How can you depend on Him more consistently?

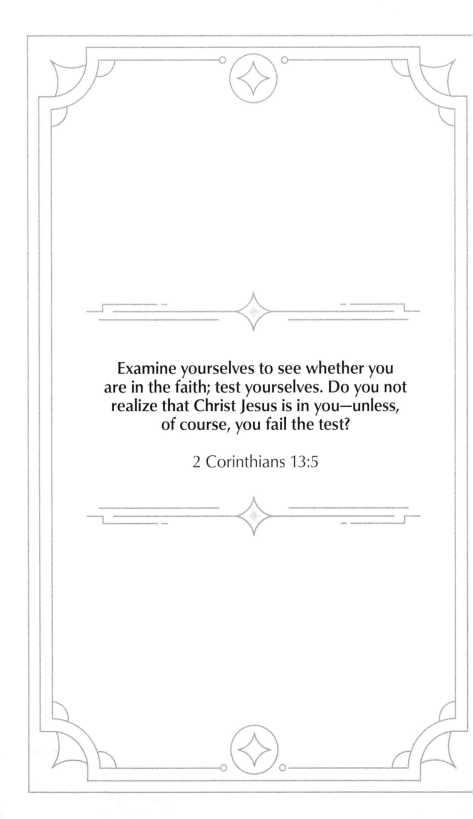

Examine yourselves to see whether you
are in the faith; test yourselves. Do you not
realize that Christ Jesus is in you—unless,
of course, you fail the test?

2 Corinthians 13:5

DAY 30

REFLECTING ON YOUR FAITH JOURNEY

You made it to the finish! As we wrap up, let's take a moment to reflect on our journey of faith and look back on how much you've grown. The apostle Paul challenges us in today's scripture to regularly reflect on our faith and recognize Jesus' presence in our lives. Reflecting on your faith journey is essential for spiritual growth. It helps you see how far you've come and identify areas where you still need to grow. Think about the times when your faith was tested and how God helped you through those challenges. These milestones show God's faithfulness and your growing trust in Him. Even if you're not yet where you want to be in your faith journey, take heart in knowing that you're not where you used to be.

Take some time this week to journal about your journey. Write down significant experiences that strengthened your faith. These could be answered prayers, difficult situations where you felt God's peace, or scriptures that spoke directly to your heart and led to a victorious breakthrough. Revisiting these memories can encourage you and remind you of God's constant power and presence in your life, always there to guide and strengthen you.

Reflecting also involves recognizing areas where you need to improve. Ask yourself if there are aspects of your life where you haven't fully trusted God or if there are habits that continue to hinder your spiritual growth. Be honest with yourself and ask God to help you in these areas. Remember, your journey of faith is unique, and each moment of reflection helps you appreciate the work God is doing in your life. Your journey is significant, and your growth is a testament to God's love and faithfulness. He will keep His promises!

The Bible says in James 1:3–4 that when your faith is tested, it leads to you being complete and fully mature as a Christian believer. Growing into full maturity as you accomplish the will of God for your life is the ultimate win. For this victory, you don't need to compete with anyone else. Jesus has won the victory already, so that's settled. The real battle is within yourself. Will you take courage and exercise the discipline it takes to be everything God has called you to be? I know you can do it, but you're the only one who can decide. Romans 8:37 reminds us, "In all these things we are more than conquerors through him who loved us." This means that no matter what challenges you face, you have the strength and power of God within you to overcome them. Whatever you face in life, you will conquer because almighty God is with you and in you.

Remember, growth in faith is a continuous journey. There will always be ups and downs, but each step brings you closer to God. Surround yourself with a good community that supports your development and encourages your faith as you encourage theirs. Celebrate your growth, learn from your challenges, and keep pressing forward. Trust that God is with you every step of the way, and let your journey be a testament to His amazing love and enduring faithfulness. The key is to keep moving forward, to keep growing, and to keep trusting in God's plan for you. Know that with God on your side, you can never lose!

PRAYER

Thank You, Lord, for bringing me this far and being faithful to see me through to the end. I thank You, Lord, for using the things that I am facing in life to bring me to full maturity as a believer. I declare that in the day of adversity, my faith will not fail. And as I win each faith battle, I will encourage others with my testimonies of Your goodness. I love You, Lord, and I thank You for always causing me to triumph! In Jesus' name, amen.

REFLECT

Write down some testimonies. How have you grown?
What areas do you still need to improve?

PRAYER

I'M WALKING IN VICTORY

I am victorious in life. I am more than a conqueror. I am a world overcomer. I overcome by the blood of the Lamb and the word of my testimony. My faith is the victory that overcomes the world.

The favor of God surrounds me like a shield. I have favor in the sight of all men. God goes before me, making the crooked places straight and opening doors that no man can shut.

I have the mind of Christ and hold the thoughts, feelings, and purposes of His heart. I have the mind of the Holy Spirit, which is life and peace. I am spiritually minded. I am living the life of the Spirit. The Holy Spirit dwells within me and directs me.

I have an unction from the Holy One and I know all things. The Holy Spirit is leading me and guiding me into all truth. He is revealing things to me and showing me things to come.

I have been born again of the incorruptible seed of the Word of God, which lives and abides forever. I am a new creation in Christ. Old things have passed away and all things have become new. I have the nature of God. I am created in His image and in His likeness. I am seated with Christ in heavenly places.

I am the righteousness of God in Christ Jesus. I am in right standing with God. I am accepted in the beloved. God loves me, and nothing can separate me from His love. I am sanctified, consecrated, and separated from the world. I am one with God. I am strong in the Lord and in the power of His might. I am empowered through my union with Him. I am anointed. I have been created by God to prosper and make a difference in this world. I am a success. I am the head. I am above only. I am blessed.

I am the redeemed of the Lord. I am redeemed from sickness and disease. I am the healed of the Lord. Sickness, disease, viruses, and infections cannot live in my body. My body is the temple of the Holy Ghost. The law of the Spirit of life in Christ Jesus flows throughout every cell, organ, and tissue of my body. By His stripes I am healed.

I am free from fear and anxiety. I fear not, for God is with me. I do not fret or have anxiety about anything. I do not have a care. I think on the good report and things worthy of praise. I believe in Jesus, and I will never be disappointed or put to shame. I let the peace of God rule in my heart, deciding and settling with finality all questions that arise in my mind.

I am being transformed by the renewing of my mind. I let the Word of God dwell in me richly. I am meditating in the Word day and night, making my way prosperous and dealing wisely in all the affairs of my life.

The Lord is my Shepherd, and I do not want. My God supplies all my needs according to His riches in glory by Christ Jesus. I am a tither, and the windows of heaven are open over my life. The blessings of the Lord are overtaking me.

No weapon formed against me shall prosper. I tread upon
serpents and scorpions and over all the works of the enemy, and
nothing shall by any means hurt me. I lay hands on the sick and
they recover. I cast out demons in Jesus' name. I take my shield
of faith, and I quench every fiery dart of the wicked one. Greater
is He who is in me than he who is in the world.

I am reigning in life as a king. I can do all things through Christ
which strengthens me. I am blessing the world with the rich,
valuable, potent resources God has placed within me. I am not
settling for less, mediocre, average, or just enough. I am only
accepting the best and the perfect will of God.

Now, thanks be unto God, who always causes me to triumph in
Christ! In Jesus' name, Amen.

Source: prayer.billwinston.org/prayer-resources

DAILY DECLARATIONS

WHO/WHAT I AM IN CHRIST

◇ I am reigning in life by Jesus Christ (Romans 5:17)

◇ I am not looking at the things that are seen, but at the things which are not seen (2 Corinthians 4:18)

◇ I am walking by faith and not by sight (2 Corinthians 5:7)

◇ I am casting down imaginations and every high thing that exalts itself against the knowledge of God (2 Corinthians 10:5)

◇ I am the righteousness of God in Christ Jesus (2 Corinthians 5:21)

◇ I am rooted and grounded in love because Christ dwells within me (Ephesians 3:17)

◇ I am the workmanship of God, created in Christ Jesus for good works (Ephesians 2:10)

◇ I am a partaker of God's divine nature (2 Peter 1:4)

◇ I am prosperous and in good health because my soul prospers (3 John 2)

◇ I am being transformed by the renewing of my mind to prove the perfect will of God (Romans 12:2)

◇ I am healed by the stripes of Jesus Christ (1 Peter 2:24)

◇ I am more than a conqueror through Jesus Christ (Romans 8:37)

◇ I am the salt of the earth and the light of the world (Matthew 5:13–14)

◇ I am complete in Christ (Colossians 2:10)

◇ I am strong in the Lord and in the power of His might (Ephesians 6:10)

◇ I am taking the shield of faith and quenching all of the fiery darts of the enemy (Ephesians 6:16)

◇ I am praying my desires and receiving them (Mark 11:24)

◇ I am like a tree planted by the rivers of water, and everything that I do prospers (Psalm 1:3)

◇ I am a temple of the Holy Ghost (1 Corinthians 6:19)

◇ I am given exceeding great and precious promises, and by them I partake of the divine nature, having escaped the corruption that is in the world through lust (2 Peter 1:4)

◇ I am led by the Spirit of God; therefore, I am a son of God (Romans 8:14)

◇ I am not walking after the flesh, but after the Spirit (Romans 8:1)

◇ I am receiving all of my needs that are met according to His riches in glory by Christ Jesus (Philippians 4:19)

◇ I am casting all of my cares upon Him because I know He cares for me (1 Peter 5:7)

- ◇ I am blessed with all spiritual blessings in Christ Jesus (Ephesians 1:3)
- ◇ I am blessed when I come in and blessed when I go out (Deuteronomy 28:6)
- ◇ I am an heir of God and a joint-heir with Jesus Christ (Romans 8:17)
- ◇ I am increasing and abounding in love (1 Thessalonians 3:12)
- ◇ I am being made perfect in every good work to do God's will (Hebrews 13:21)
- ◇ I am showing forth the praise of God (Psalm 51:15)

Source: livingwd.org/lwcc-prayers-and-confessions/

ABOUT THE AUTHOR

David S. Winston serves as a pastor at Living Word Christian Center, Forest Park, Illinois, and served as youth pastor of the Go Hard for Christ Youth Ministry for over fifteen years. He also serves as the international director of Bill Winston Ministries, a worldwide outreach ministry. He is a bestselling author, international speaker, and the founder of Winston Leadership Institute. David empowers people of all ages to be everything God has called them to be. He lives in the Chicagoland area with his wife, Niki, and they have four children altogether.

Instagram: @davidswinston
Facebook: davidswinston
X: @davidswinston
YouTube.com/davidswinston

ADDITIONAL BOOKS BY DAVID S. WINSTON
Authentic: The Confidence to be Yourself,
the Courage to Release Your Greatness
Strong in Spirit: 5-minute Devotions for Preteen Boys

www.Davidswinston.com

Printed in the USA
CPSIA information can be obtained
at www.ICGtesting.com
CBHW051634171024
15995CB00016B/1563